CHARACTERS

James Wormald
Iris Wormald
Marigold Barker
Ken Smedley
Thelma Smedley
Edgar Baldock

The action takes place in the living-room and patio of James Wormald's bungalow

ACT I, Scene 1   Saturday morning
      Scene 2   Evening, several days later

ACT II, Scene 1   The following morning
      Scene 2   The same afternoon

Time—the present

ACT I

SCENE 1

The living-room, patio and garden fence of a bungalow in a provincial green belt. Saturday morning

The bungalow has been furnished with a total lack of individuality but with supposed good taste from the reproductions department of a furnishing store. There are doors leading to the entrance hall and the kitchen. The patio, which is a recent addition to the bungalow, is situated beyond the french windows

James Wormald, his wife, Iris, and their married daughter, Marigold, are having breakfast on the patio. They are eating Cornflakes, the packet of which is on the table. There is complete silence until they have finished.

James has been thinking heavily during breakfast

James I'm not quite sure. What do you think, Marigold?

Marigold It's difficult. What do you think, Mother?

Iris I'm open-minded. Why don't we let your father decide?

James (*jokingly*) Come along, Iris! Be positive!

Iris (*positively*) All right then, I'll tell you what I'd like . . . (*Losing confidence*) Although when we had them before we left half.

James The Rice Crispies?

Iris Yes.

James Hmmm. (*A pause*) What's wrong with Wheat Flakes?

Marigold Nothing.

Iris Nothing.

James (*reluctantly*) Shall we agree on Wheat Flakes?

Marigold Yes.

Iris Although we were going to give the All-Bran a try again. Last Sunday. We were having breakfast in the living room. When we had all that rain. And you said, why don't we give the All-Bran a try again?

James We could give the All-Bran a try again.

Iris Or Wheat Flakes.

James Or Wheat Flakes.

Marigold Of course, what you can get are the individual packets. I used to get them when I was living in Stevenage. Harold enjoyed them. Eight individual packets. Rice Crispies, Cornflakes, Wheat Flakes and Sugar Snax, Honey Puffs, etc.

James Personal selection?

Marigold Yes.

James We'll give that a try.

Iris Not the All-Bran?

James Or the All-Bran.

Iris I'll tell you what we'll do. We'll all think about it.

Iris puts some of the breakfast things on to a tray and takes them into the kitchen.

Marigold studies the Cornflakes packet. James, filling his pipe, looks over the fence

James They haven't started unloading yet.

Marigold They'll have gone for breakfast. They must have set off at the crack of dawn if they've come up from Rugby.

James We've no evidence that they have come up from Rugby. The furniture van comes from Rugby, but that doesn't signify that Rugby was the point of departure.

Marigold It would be somewhere in the radius though, wouldn't it?

James Oh, it'd be somewhere in the radius.

Marigold You wouldn't order a furniture van from Rugby if you lived in—well . . .

James Brighton.

Marigold Brighton. Yes. It'll be somewhere in the radius. (*Holding up the packet*) Have you seen this?

James (*cynically*) Another unrepeatable offer, I don't doubt.

Marigold This one really is. (*Reading*) Listen to this. "This luxury garden hammock in unbreakable polystyrene-foam-filled, wipe-clean cushions in three colours—beautiful, fade-resistant fringed canopy . . ."

James Yours for two packet tops.

Marigold Three. Plus cheque or money order for twenty-three pounds fifty.

James Rubbish.

Marigold You haven't even looked at it. I think it's quite attractive.

James Plastic rubbish.

Marigold Don't be so dogmatic, Father.

James Dogmatism doesn't enter it. I know what the British manufacturer can provide for twenty-three pounds fifty—irrespective of packet tops—and I want no part or parcel of it in my home. You continue to amaze me, Marigold.

Marigold You can't condemn a product sight unseen.

James Neither can you tell a book by its cover. I would have thought past experience would have taught you that.

Marigold (*changing the subject, looking over the fence*) You never took their flowering cherry.

James No, I've missed that golden opportunity. I didn't like to, to tell you the truth.

Marigold They said you could have it.

James We've got to consider the larger picture. Consider our new neighbours. As prospective purchasers they're shown over the bungalow, presumably. They see a flowering cherry in their prospective garden. They plonk down their deposit and they move in from Rugby, or

WHOOPS-A-DAISY

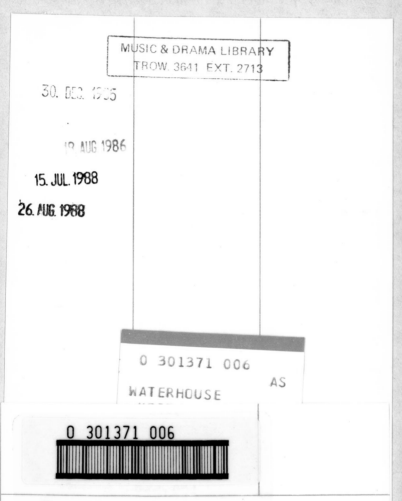

WILTSHIRE LIBRARY & MUSEUM SERVICE

Headquarters : Bythesea Road, Trowbridge.

Items should be returned to the library from which they were borrowed on or before the date stamped above, unless a renewal has been granted.

ISBN 0 573 11486 2

round that area. And lo and behold, the blessed tree's jumped over the fence and is flourishing right in the middle of my lawn. There'd be a lot of explaining to do. It wouldn't get us off on the right foot.

Marigold It was given to you. All you've got to do is tell them.

James I don't like telling people things. I prefer to wait till I'm asked.

Marigold Take the tree now, then wait till you're asked.

James That would give an impression of guilt. At the sacrifice of a flowering cherry tree, I prefer to nurture my peace of mind.

Iris comes back for the rest of the breakfast things

Iris They haven't started unloading yet.

James Marigold tells me the men have gone off for breakfast.

Iris I told *her* that. They've come all the way from Rugby—they must have set off at the crack of dawn.

Marigold Father thinks they're not from Rugby at all.

James Within the radius. We agreed on that.

Iris It says Rugby on the van.

James (*picking up the Cornflakes packet*) It says unrepeatable offer on that Cornflakes packet but I beg leave to differ. If there's one thing I've learned in this life, it's never judge a book by its cover. (*He walks into the living-room*)

Iris You know who your father's referring to, don't you?

Marigold He's bringing up Harold again.

Iris Oh, no. He's bringing up Bradshaw.

Marigold I thought he was talking about Harold.

Iris I thought he was talking about Bradshaw.

They go into the living-room

James (*putting the Cornflakes on the sideboard*) You know who I'm referring to now, don't you? Bradshaw.

Iris There you are.

James (*to Marigold*) You never met Bradshaw.

Marigold You told me about him.

Iris It was while you were in Stevenage.

James I was considering taking a partner into the business. I was introduced to Bradshaw, a man of apparently impeccable means. He even took me to the bank with him, showed me his statement. Three thousand pounds in the black. We drew up the articles of association and then blow me down, it turned out he hadn't a penny to bless himself with.

Iris He owed it all to the Inland Revenue.

James And sundry creditors. And where did that leave me? I'd ordered costly die-stamping machinery that I couldn't pay for. I'd re-tooled my Crabtree Press for colour printing. I'd ordered whole new founts of type. I was almost ruined. I had to draw from capital, you know.

Iris No holidays that year.

James Just the week in Bournemouth. Still, we survived. But there is a moral there somewhere. Never judge a book by its cover. When I've got a free moment at the shop I might print that on a card, and you may hang it in your bedroom. Never judge a book by its cover.

Iris You know who your father's referring to now, don't you?

James You know who I'm referring to now, don't you?

Iris He's referring to Harold now.

Marigold I know. And I don't think we should bring up Harold at breakfast-time.

Iris I'd prefer not to bring up Harold ever again. It's over now.

James But it's not over. There's the divorce yet.

Iris It's no use burying your head in the sand, Marigold.

James *And* all the attendant publicity.

Iris And we have *finished* breakfast, Marigold. We've got to discuss these things sooner or later.

James Exactly.

Iris Half-past nine! And I haven't vacuumed the front bedroom yet.

James It's time I potted those geraniums. They won't pot themselves.

Marigold There's nothing to discuss.

James (*making for the patio*) There's a great deal to discuss.

Iris (*at the kitchen door*) And better sooner than later.

Marigold There won't be any publicity. Harold isn't defending the divorce.

James (*returning*) That makes not a jot of difference. You'll be called upon to attend.

Iris (*returning, anxiously*) It's only a token attendance . . .

James It is not a token attendance. She has to present evidence. In court. In public.

Marigold The solicitor said the newspapers can't report the evidence.

James But you've still got to give it! In a public court. The day will come when you'll have to stand up and announce to every Tom, Dick and Harry that you were married to a man of certain habits.

An awkward pause

Iris (*tidying up the newspaper rack*) Marigold, have you taken the *Woman's Own* into your room?

Marigold I haven't seen it this week, Mother.

Iris Do you know, I think they've forgotten to deliver it again.

James And the *Amateur Gardener*. That's the second time that's happened. I shall step down to that newsagent's and take it up with him. This morning.

Iris You have it out with him. Then at least you'll have cleared the air.

James It's always the best policy. We've certainly cleared the air in our own home. We've achieved something today.

Iris It's not as if she knew about his certain habits when she married him. How could she? He was like anyone else at the meal table.

Marigold He had very good table manners.

James So did Hitler. It's no good trying to whitewash him, Marigold.

Iris She doesn't want to whitewash him. Quite the reverse. She wants a divorce.

James Exactly my point. It's no good trying to whitewash him. The truth will out. He was a man of admitted certain habits, and as such should be brought to book. It's not only Marigold that must be considered, do you see? He forces his certain habits upon her. No doubt, given opportunity, he'll force his certain habits on the next.

Iris That's nothing to do with us. Leave well alone.

James I agree with you. Any public-spirited divorce judge is going to insist that Harold's certain habits are made public! What I'm driving at is, how can we keep out of it?

Marigold I do have to appear in court.

James But give them the minimal amount of information under cross-examination. Just enough to satisfy the court and see justice done.

Iris What Father is saying is that you don't have to go into every little detail.

James You see, there's the question of the time when she was taken ill.

Iris She doesn't have to tell them about that.

James Exactly my point. Don't discuss the subject.

Marigold I wasn't even with Harold when I was taken ill.

James Quite so. But truth will out. And you have to admit that your illness was a direct result of your leaving Harold.

Iris She doesn't have to mention her illness at all. That's just between us.

Marigold It's my own personal business.

James Wrong, Marigold. Your illness was a family affair. We were all concerned, in one way or another. But there's no reason why it should go beyond the family. No reason why it should be brought up—in court.

Iris Don't tell them more than is necessary.

James Just the minimum. And you could take that as a general principle in life. Never go half-way to meet trouble.

Iris Keep yourself to yourself.

James And never judge a book by its cover.

Iris It's the way we've always tried to live.

James We won't pursue the subject, Iris. Enough said is enough said. Man hath but a short time to live, and we've wasted enough time this morning.

Iris I wouldn't exactly say wasted, James.

James Not exactly wasted. True. Possibly well-spent. Will anybody be using the bathroom this morning?

Iris For how long?

James That's what I'm enquiring. (*Looking out of the window*) Hulloa! They've started, then.

Iris (*also peering*) They must have finished their breakfast.

Marigold (*joining them*) They'll find they've got difficulties with that settee. There's only one wall a settee like that will fit and that's along there. (*She indicates a wall in their own bungalow*)

Iris You can't put a settee under a serving hatch.

Marigold That's what I'm saying. It's the only place it will fit.

Iris They'll have difficulties with that.

James They might not put it by the wall. They might place it informally across the middle of the floor. Over there.

Iris That'd be unusual.

James Not unheard of. The whole world doesn't place its settees along a wall.

Marigold Everybody in our Crescent does. From what I've observed.

James By looking in at the windows, no doubt. And then you wonder why they look in at ours. (*Turning from the window*) Well, will anybody?

Iris Will anybody what?

James Be using the bathroom. This morning.

Iris I might go in.

James How long for?

Marigold Not for long?

Iris (*embarrassed*) I shouldn't think so.

Marigold Because I was thinking of using it.

Iris Oh, I shan't be that long.

James You mean you'll just be popping in?

Iris Yes.

James And out again.

Iris Yes. (*Looking out of the window*) That must be their sideboard.

Marigold I couldn't live with that.

James To each his own, Marigold. How long will you be using it for?

Marigold Not long.

James Not just popping in?

Marigold No, longer than that.

James Five minutes? Twenty minutes?

Marigold Something like that.

James I see.

Iris Why are you asking? Did you want to go in?

James Not precisely. (*To Marigold*) Will you be using the bath taps at all?

Marigold I hadn't considered the bath taps.

James It comes down to the question of opening the bathroom window. I might require to run the garden hose through the window. I thought I might do some watering along the borders.

Marigold Oh. Yes, you can use the bath taps, by all means.

Iris I think your father was querying the window, Marigold.

Marigold You can have the window.

James Open?

Marigold Yes.

James It won't inconvenience you?

Marigold I only want the bathroom sink.

James You'll be using the sink?

Marigold Only to wash some things.

James Ah. Then you won't have recourse to lock the bathroom door?

Marigold Why should I?

James I was only enquiring.

Marigold I should think I could lock the bathroom door in my own home if I want some privacy!

Iris There's no need to snap your father's head off, Marigold!

Marigold It's no business of his!

James I happen to recall one occasion when it *was* my business, Marigold.

Iris Your father's talking about when you were taken ill.

Marigold I've no intention of being taken ill this morning.

Iris Your father found it necessary to break the bathroom door in.

James We won't pursue the subject, Iris. Just so long as we know what's happening.

Iris And we all know where we stand.

Iris exits to the kitchen

The doorbell rings. James and Marigold exchange a surprised glance

Marigold Somebody's ringing our bell.

James Yes.

Iris The front door-bell.

Marigold It can't be the groceries.

James I'm wondering if it isn't the Jehovah's Witnesses.

Iris appears at the kitchen door

Iris Wasn't that our front door-bell?

Marigold (*whispering*) We think it's the Jehovah's Witnesses.

Iris (*whispering*) Let it ring. They'll go away.

Iris goes back into the kitchen

James They're a blessed nuisance. I'd like to hear of a religious sect whose precept is that an Englishman's home is his castle. If it's not Jehovah's Witnesses it's Mormons and if it's not Mormons it's the First Church of Christ, Scientist . . .

During the above Ken Smedley enters along the path at the side of the house. He now stands on the patio looking in at the french windows. He wears a corduroy cap and a blazer with a regimental badge. He knocks tentatively on the window frame

Marigold sees him, but not James

Marigold Father . . .

James We were plagued by Anglican nuns during your Stevenage days. You never heard the full story of that, did you?

Marigold Someone at the—er . . .

Smedley Good morning.

James Good morning?

Smedley Sorry to interrupt your week-end. I'm looking for a telephone.

James Ah, well let me direct you. If you go to the end of the Crescent, cross over to the parade of shops, there's a box just outside . . .

Smedley (*smiling, shaking his head*) I'd never find it. I'm a total stranger. I was wondering if I could use yours.

James My phone?

Smedley Yes.

James My telephone?

Smedley Yes.

James It's—er—what one would term an emergency?
Smedley Oh, no.

James looks at Marigold for help, which is not forthcoming

   I ought to introduce myself. We're moving in next door.
James (*the light dawning*) I see. Ah, well that throws a completely new
   light . . . Forgive my rudeness, we weren't quite sure who . . .
Smedley I did ring the bell. I thought it must be out of order.
Marigold We thought you were a Witness.
Smedley A what?
James Jehovah's Witness.
Marigold There's a lot of them about. Especially at week-ends.
Smedley Thanks for the tip.
James (*now relaxed*) I got the impression that we must be having new
   neighbours. We've just been watching your furniture going in.
Marigold We couldn't help noticing the van.
Smedley Yes. It's a long job.
James Very tiring.
Marigold You'll be glad when you're settled in.
Smedley (*indicating the telephone*) Is it all right if I . . . ?
James By all means.
Smedley (*picking up the telephone*) It's only a local call.
Marigold Would you like us to, er . . . ?
Smedley It's nothing private.
James We're quite prepared to, er . . . ?
Smedley Just carry on as normal. (*He dials a number*)

   Iris enters

Iris I've finished using the bathroom if . . . Oh.
James This is our new neighbour. Mr . . .
Smedley Ken, Ken Smedley.
James How do you do, Mr Smedley. My wife, Mrs Wormald. My
   daughter . . .

*But Smedley has turned his attention to the telephone, where his call has
been answered*

Smedley (*on the telephone*) Ernie? . . . Ken . . . Yes! It is! . . . Ha ha ha!
   (*A loud braying laugh*) I thought we'd catch you with your trousers down!
   Ha ha ha! . . . No, we set off early, you see. Crack of dawn.

Marigold and Iris exchange a significant glance

   Did you manage to get it for me? . . . What? . . . Did he? . . . He
   swallowed it, did he? Ha ha ha! (*Another braying laugh*)

*Ernie, at the other end, is telling him a funny story and the rest of the tele-
phone call is occupied by Smedley laughing and listening, and occasionally
interjecting a word*

   . . . So what did you say? . . . No! . . . Ha ha ha! . . . And what did

George say?... Ha ha ha!... I bet that surprised you!... Ha ha ha! Well, I won't keep you now, Ernie. We'll be in touch.... What's that? ... Ha ha ha ha ha! Seven-five-two-six-nine-three-four. (*He puts the receiver down*) He'll say anything over a telephone.

Iris Oh, yes?

Smedley I have to laugh. (*He proffers a coin to James*) Thank you very much.

James Oh, there's no need for that.

Smedley Take it.

James No, really ...

Smedley stuffs the coin into James's breast pocket

Smedley It all adds up. Twenty five 'p's' make a pound. Well, I'd better go and see how the heavy gang are getting on. I'll say cheerio, then. Cheerio.

James Cheerio.

Marigold Cheerio.

Smedley (*to Iris*) Cheerio.

Iris (*forced into it*) Cheerio.

Smedley leaves by the front door

After a moment, James peers round the door to make sure he has gone

James Well!

Iris So it wasn't the Jehovah's Witnesses.

James I'd rather it had been. What a thoroughly obnoxious man!

Marigold You mustn't judge a book by its cover. I though he was quite pleasant. Quite humorous. Quite polite.

James I've said it before, Marigold, you have a peculiar yard-stick when it comes to standards of personal etiquette.

Iris Manners maketh man.

James Your mother knows what I mean.

Iris He had his hat on.

James Cap. All the time.

Iris He never took it off. And he didn't raise it when we were introduced.

Marigold You don't raise your hat is somebody's house.

James You don't *wear* your hat in somebody's house. The point I'm making.

Marigold Perhaps he forgot.

James In the presence of ladies? Uncouth, that's the term I'd apply to that gentleman. And I'll tell you something else now. I'm talking about his eyes, now, and his mouth. Do you know who he reminded me of?

Iris You know who your father means, Marigold?

Marigold I haven't a notion.

James (*to Iris*) *I* have a notion, though, and so has Mother.

Iris Very strong resemblance. Very marked.

Marigold He's not a bit like Harold.

Iris There you are, you did notice.

Marigold He's not like Harold at all.

James Well, likeness or no likeness. I don't think we need concern ourselves with friend Smedley any further this morning. Or, for that matter,
in the future.

Iris But he's going to live next door.

James (*looking out from the patio into Smedley's garden*) He may live
where he pleases—my threshold is sacrosant. (*He gives a self-satisfied
guffaw*) This'll interest Marigold.

Iris It's a garden swing.

James Correction. Hammock. As advertised on the backs of Cornflakes
packets. And that blue-and-white monstrosity is what Marigold would
have had me purchase! (*To Marigold*) There's the arbiter of your good
taste, Marigold! Well-mannered, good-humoured Brother Smedley,
who equips his garden on twenty-three pounds fifty and three packet
tops. I wouldn't be surprised if he'd furnished his whole house on
packet tops. Not like Harold? He's a carbon copy. Well, let that be a
lesson, that's all. Consider that every morning. Plastic hammocks might
do for Rugby and Stevenage but we can manage without them up here.
And we can manage very well without Brother Smedley.

Iris I hope you've listened to your father. There's no need for any dealings
with that man at all. We shall keep ourselves to ourselves, as we always
have done.

The telephone rings. Marigold answers it

Marigold Seven-five-two-six-nine-three-four? ... Would you just hold
the line a moment? (*To James*) It's for him.

Iris Who?

Marigold points towards the Smedley bungalow

James If that doesn't take the biscuit. How's that for blatant effrontery?

Marigold What shall I say?

James I'll deal with this. (*He takes the telephone*) Seven-five-two-six-nine-
three-four, Mr Wormald speaking. ... I see. ... Would you just hold
the line for a moment. ... (*He puts his hand over the receiver*). Well,
I don't know. What can you say?

Marigold That is going too far! Slam the phone down. I would.

James Yes, I noticed you doing so. I suppose I'd better go fetch him.

Iris You can't refuse, really.

James (*into the telephone*) Would you hold the line for a moment?

James puts the receiver down and goes out

*Marigold walks over to the receiver and deliberately speaks so that she
might be heard.*

Marigold All I can say is that some people have a nerve.

Iris makes an agitated shushing gesture and motions towards the telephone

*Smedley barges in, followed by James. He winks broadly at the two
women, goes and picks up the telephone as if he owned it*

Smedley Smedley . . . George! I've just this minute put the phone down on Ernie. What did he say? . . . He didn't! Ha ha ha ha! So what's the upshot then? . . . (*with a sudden switch of mood*) What do you mean, they can't? . . . (*He frowns as he listens but, as he catches Iris's eye, he makes a kissing gesture in her direction. Angrily on the telephone*) Tell them to get off their arses and get cracking! . . . (*Changing his mood again*) All right, Georgie-Porgie, I'll leave it with you. How's Mary? . . . Ha ha ha! Well don't overdo it, both of you . . . Ta-ra.

Smedley puts the telephone down and strides out on to the patio. The Wormald family watch him.

(*calling across*) Thelma! THELMA! The bastards have let us down again! . . . All right! . . . Whoops-a-daisy! Don't drop that crockery!

James Well!

Iris Well!

Marigold Well!

Smedley Well!

Smedley walks back into the living-room and stands proprietorially in front of the fireplace. He surveys the room. The Wormalds survey him

About sixteen grand, eh?

James I beg your pardon?

Smedley What you paid. For this place. 'Bout sixteen thousand pounds.

James (*cautiously*) We have been here a number of years.

Iris Since—oh—nineteen fifty-three, wasn't it, Marigold?

Smedley Ah! You'd have had a snip in them days. Three thousand? Four thousand.

James The bungalows were new then. They were asking three thousand seven hundred. (*For Iris's benefit: he is not giving a secret away*) They *were* widely advertised at that price.

Smedley You'd get sixteen grand now, with the right agent. (*Nodding towards the telephone*) You won't mind about the phone calls—there might be a couple more?

James (*doubtfully*) Not at all.

Marigold Although we were thinking of going out. Mother?

Iris We were thinking about it.

Smedley Well, if you're out, you're out. I won't ask you for the key because I don't know you well enough. Ha ha ha. (*He looks pointedly at James*)

James One of us should be in. I don't think we shall all be going out.

Smedley That's all right then. Well, we're not having bad weather for it. Not bad at all.

James Very mild. For the time of year.

Smedley Would you think so? Last year we never saw a cloud before September.

Iris Last year was beautiful. We went to Bournemouth.

James Normally we go to the Costa del Sol.

Smedley Mark you, last year was exceptional.

Iris Very exceptional.

Smedley You don't often get it sunny as late as this.

James Not often.

Smedley Although it's sunny now.

James Very pleasant.

Smedley So you can say this year is exceptional as well.

James Well, I'd say that. An exceptional year. Wouldn't you say that, Iris?

Iris Very exceptional.

Smedley Who's the artistic one in the family?

Marigold It's a reproduction.

Smedley I might have guessed. I can see you're fond of a good painting. I don't think I caught the name?

Iris Mrs Barker.

Smedley Oh, not Wormald.

Iris She was a Wormald. And then she married. She became a Barker.

Smedley Woof-woof! Ha ha ha! Can I use your lavatory?

Iris The bathroom?

Smedley I wouldn't ask, only we haven't had a chance yet to rig ours out with the accoutrements. Toilet paper and such forth.

James Yes, of course. I'll . . .

Smedley (*going to the door*) Don't bother. I'll find it.

Smedley goes out

There is an awkward silence as the Wormalds exchange glances

James Well, then. I'd say that was rather a personal request.

Marigold I'd call it an imposition.

James I suppose, under the circumstances . . .

Iris We had to offer.

Marigold I don't see why we should.

Iris You've *got* to, Marigold. Supposing it was you? I wouldn't like to think of you in a strange house wanting to . . . (*She checks herself*)

James Under the circumstances, it was the only thing we *could* do.

Iris Sssssssshhh!

Smedley enters. He has forgotten to fasten his flies and his shirt is plainly visible

The two women avert their eyes and eventually, with pleading, agitated glances, draw James's attention to the cause of their distress

Smedley Did you do all that yourself?

James What would that be, Mr Smedley?

Smedley The decor in the loo. The tiling.

James We have made certain structural alterations throughout the bungalow.

Smedley I see you have. I don't miss a lot. (*Tapping his forehead*) It all goes on up here. (*To Marigold, abruptly*) Are you bereaved?

Marigold, unable to address Smedley in his present state, looks beseechingly at James, who now notices Smedley's dress

James Oh. Mr Smedley . . .

Smedley I haven't put my foot in it, have I?

James (*desperately*) I wonder if you'd like me to show you the kitchen. I've made certain structural alterations there too.

Smedley I'd like to have a look-see at the whole billet, eventually. Might get some ideas. (*To Marigold*) I hope I didn't touch on a raw nerve just then?

James (*trying to take Smedley's arm*) And then we have the patio out here.

Smedley Quite nice. Quite nice.

James Mr Smedley . . . (*He whispers something*)

Smedley Come again.

James (*desperately*) I rather think you've forgotten to adjust your dress.

Smedley (*following James's gaze*) Whoops-a-daisy. (*He fastens his zip cheerfully*) A case of locking the stable door after the horse has gone. (*To Marigold*) No, I was saying. I thought I might have jumped in at the deep end. Enquiring about your husband.

Iris Marigold is staying with us. For the present. ⎱ *Speaking*

James Yes. Most of the structural alterations I have effected ⎰ *together*
myself.

Smedley (*looking at the patio*) Nice bit of paving, that.

James (*proudly*) The Spanish patio.

Smedley I thought it must be.

James A faithful replica of a villa I admired on the Costa del Sol.

Smedley I should imagine you enjoyed the odd siesta out there?

Iris And breakfast.

James Weekend breakfasts. Weather permitting, of course.

Smedley Very continental!

James We like to think so.

Smedley Very contemporary.

James Quite contemporary. A little lacking in privacy, unfortunately. We have, on occasion, found ourselves being watched.

Marigold Rosedene.

Iris And Mon Repos.

James Yes. Mon Repos are *your* immediate opposite neighbours.

Marigold Their bedroom windows overlook our patio.

James He's the worst offender. I've noticed him twice. In a dressing-gown.

Iris Peeping through the bedroom curtains.

Smedley Sounds a funny sort of bloke.

Iris We don't speak to them.

James We like to keep ourselves to ourselves. The sanctity of the home. It's very difficult. You'll find you'll have a lot of callers.

Iris Jehovah's Witnesses. Regular as clockwork.

Marigold Salvation Army, Sundays.

James At one point we found ourselves plagued by Anglican nuns.

Smedley's reaction to all the above is a little absent as he is methodically

B

*prying through the Wormalds' things, picking up books and other objects,
looking at them and putting them down in the wrong place*

Iris Mark you, they're entitled to their views.

James Oh, they're entitled to their views. What I resent is their intrusion
into my privacy. And the assumption of any Tom, Dick or Harry who
turns up on my doorstep, that I'm prepared to divulge my religious
persuasion.

*Smedley, who has plainly not been listening, loses interest in the Wormalds'
objets d'art*

Smedley You're not Catholics, are you?

James (*promptly*) C. of E.

Smedley You don't mind Catholic gags, then?

The Wormalds look at him blankly

Jokes.

Iris (*anxiously*) We're quite broadminded.

Smedley You'll enjoy this one. Don't look so worried, it's clean. (*Nodding
at Marigold*) She's disappointed, for a start. Aren't you? Eh?

A weak smile from Marigold

Hang about a bit, sweetie, I've got one for you later . . .

*During Smedley's joke his wife, Thelma, enters along the path and via
the patio into the living-room. She is carrying a tray laden with tea things.
As she cannot interrupt Smedley's joke she waits patiently with her tray*

*James, Iris and Marigold cast furtive glances at her to which she responds
with a frank, homely smile*

Anyway, there was these two what-is-it, cardinals, in the Vatican. And
one of them's in church, you know, worshipping, having a pray, and he
looks up, like, and lo and behold there's Our Lord Jesus Christ. In
person. Beard, robes, sandals, full house. He's just wandering about,
giving the place the once-over. So. This cardinal goes to find his mate
and tells him, I can't do the accent so I won't attempt it, he says, "Hey,
Whoops-a-daisy! Jesus is here." He says, "You what?" He says, "I'm
telling you, Jesus is here." He says, "He isn't, is he?" He says, "He is."
So. The other one says, "Well there's only one thing to do," he says,
"we've got to tell the Pope." So off they go to look for his Eminence,
and he's standing out on his balcony blessing the crowd. And this
cardinal tugs at his, you know, and the Pope says out of the corner of
his mouth, I can't really do the accent, he says, "Go-a-da-way, I'm
blessing-a-da peoples." So this cardinal says, "Yes but your Holiness,
Our Lord Jesus Christ is among us." And the Pope says, "I know, you
bloody fool, look busy."

*The Wormalds titter politely and look at Thelma, awaiting some explanation
of her presence*

Thelma (*to Smedley*) I told you they would and they have.

Smedley They've not broken it!

Thelma nods

> *Smedley, with a heavy sigh of exasperation, gets up and goes out to see the removal men, through the patio*

Thelma serenely pours tea, completely at home in the Wormalds' house

Thelma The funny thing is, I knew they were going to. I said before we set off, if there's one thing that's going to get broken it's that dressing-table mirror. (*To Iris, handing her a cup of tea*) One lump or two?
Iris Oh. Two, thank you.
Thelma It juts out at an angle, you see. It sort of comes down in a fluted effect. (*To James, handing him a cup of tea*). One lump or two?
James One, thank you.
Thelma (*to Marigold*) And what about you, love? One lump or two?
Marigold No sugar, thank you.
Thelma Slimming? I wouldn't have thought you'd need to.

Marigold smiles politely. Thelma is about to hand her the cup of tea, but hesitates

> Just a minute, I think I've sugared it.
Marigold It doesn't matter.
Thelma Are you sure? I've only put one lump in.
Marigold It's quite all right.
Thelma I can pour it out and give you some fresh. It's no trouble.
Marigold No. Really.
Thelma Are you sure? (*To Iris*) Is she sure?
Iris She can take sugar.
Thelma She's only got to say the word. Now. Who can I force a biscuit on? (*She offers one to Iris*)
Iris (*with a tight smile*) No thank you.
Thelma Go on, get one down you. Take two. *Take two.* I shall be very offended if you don't take two. (*Turning to James*) Take two.

The telephone rings. James, encumbered by cup, saucer and plate, attempts to rise

> *Smedley strides in and picks up the telephone*

James, astonished by this, slumps back in his seat

Smedley Hello? . . . Am I still interested in what? . . . (*To James*) Whoops-a-daisy, I thought it was for me. My best apologies.

James is struggling to rise again but Smedley waves him back

> (*to James*) It's nothing personal. Somebody wants to know if you're interested in his motor mower.
James (*succeeding in rising, and handing his cup and plate to Iris*) It's about the small ad I replied to.
Smedley Are you interested?

James (*going to the telephone*) That depends, of course, on the condition . . .
Smedley (*into the telephone*) Is it in good nick ? . . . (*To James*) It's in good
nick. What's he asking for it ?

James reaches the telephone, but Smedley has no intention of handing it over

James Fifty pounds.
Smedley What make is it?
James An Ajax. Quite a bargain.
Smedley (*into the phone*) Hang on . . . (*To James*) He's seen you coming.
(*Into the telephone*) Mr Wormald may be in the market if you're open to
offers . . .

Thelma hands Smedley a cup of tea, and he mouths her a few kisses

(*Into the telephone*) If you had another customer, friend, you wouldn't
be ringing me. . . . Now we're on the same wave-length. Come down a
bit. . . . Now, don't give me all that. We both know what a second-hand
Ajax will fetch. . . . Hang on hang on—thirteen quid, final offer. (*To
James*) Can you collect tomorrow?

James nods

(*Into the telephone*) You're on. Happy? Good lad. (*To James, replacing
the telephone*) You've got a bargain.
James I'm most grateful.
Smedley So am I. I'll be round to borrow it every Saturday. (*With a wink
at Iris*) My little joke. (*Back to James*) It's a pity we're not in Rugby. I
had a contact there—mowers, rollers, rustic fences, garden furniture—
the lot.
Marigold (*with a smirk at James*) We noticed your garden hammock.
Smedley Same feller. I got that at cost. Forty-eight pounds across any
counter. Go on, take a look.

James and Iris peer dutifully out

To me—guess. You won't guess. Only twenty-eight quid. I'll get him to
send you a gnome on appro. (*He drains his tea and glares at Thelma*)
Are you ready? (*To the Wormalds*) Just a quickie. Gather round. West
Indian and a Hebrew gent. Waiting for a bus. Coloured bloke says, I
can't do the accent, "What time's the next bus due?" So the Hebrew says
"I don't know, you black bastard." (*To Iris*) You shouldn't have been
listening to that. (*To Thelma*) Come on.

Smedley breezes out through the patio, Thelma follows him

James Well!
Iris Well!
Marigold All I can say is, some people!
Iris (*looking at her cup and saucer*) We've still got their cups.
Marigold (*putting her cup and saucer down as far away as possible*) I'm
certainly not taking them back.

James Live and let live, Marigold.

Iris (*examining her own cup*) This one's got a crack.

Marigold Pushing themselves in like that!

James (*to them both*) Their ways may not be our ways. Different people have different attitudes to life. (*To Marigold*) You must surely have noticed that when you were living in Stevenage, Marigold. A pair of rough diamonds, let's all agree on that. I think we can also assume that their hearts are in the right place.

Marigold They'll be living out of our pockets if we let them.

Iris Not if we keep ourselves to ourselves. And credit where credit is due, Marigold. Mr Smedley did save your father several pounds on the motor mower.

James Quite an astute man, Mr Smedley. Mark you, I'll say this. I don't think he's invariably got the edge on me when it comes to a bargain. How much did he pay for his garden hammock?

Marigold Twenty-eight pounds.

James And how much is our unrepeatable offer?

Marigold Twenty-three pounds fifty.

Iris Plus three packet tops.

James (*picking up the Cornflakes packet*) I think that solves the cereal question for next week. Cornflakes it is. (*He tears out the coupon and the Cornflakes spill on the floor*) Whoops-a-daisy!

CURTAIN

SCENE 2

The same. Several days later, about eight p.m.

The garden hammock—£23.50 plus three packet tops—is now installed on the patio. James and Iris are out. Marigold, whose skirt is rather long, is taking advantage of their absence to see how she would look in a shorter one. She lays her knitting machine aside and hitches her skirt up over her knees, then— daringly—even higher. She practises sitting down and crossing her knees with her skirt at various lengths. She finally hits on a fairly seductive pose which pleases her. She hears the front door open and hastily takes up her knitting-machine. James and Iris enter. They have had a little to drink and are fractionally noisier than usual, and a little bit giggly

James It's as I say. Remain receptive and you'll learn something new every day.

Iris I never thought I'd take to the taste of spirits. I always thought spirits wouldn't agree with me.

James They seem to have agreed with you this evening. You were very high-spirited!

Iris I do like the way they've done their bathroom. I like the tile effect.

James Of course, that bathroom lacked only one thing. Do you know what it lacked? It lacked an army boot.

Iris (*with a giggle*) Really, James!

James I'm still chuckling over that one. (*To Marigold*) Ken was telling us
something about his army experiences. Apparently he was very ill one
evening—he'd had a little too much to drink. And there he was in bed—
in his pit—and he was feeling very ill indeed. The bathroom was some
distance away and so, apparently, he did no more than take the boot of
one of his colleagues and used it as a receptacle.

Marigold is not amused—pointedly

James Of course, you'd have to hear him tell it to appreciate the story.

Iris It was a very pleasant evening.

James Most stimulating.

Iris Very amusing.

James *Very* pleasant evening. (*To Marigold*) I hope you realize that you
ruined it completely?

Iris Ken and Thelma were most offended, Marigold.

Marigold I told you I didn't want to go.

James But you didn't tell your hosts. It was left to your mother and me to
make your excuses.

Iris We said you had a headache—

James —just for future reference.

Marigold I have got a headache. I've had it all evening.

James There is such a thing as being neighbourly, Marigold.

Marigold There is such a thing as spending an evening at home.

James Moping.

Marigold I haven't been moping.

James You're always moping. Isn't she always moping, Mother?

Iris I've said it to her time and time again: Marigold, for goodness' sake
stop moping.

James You quite put a damper on our evening.

Marigold Why should it worry you if I choose to stay in?

James I might remind you that we left you alone on a previous occasion,
Marigold.

Iris Your father's talking about the time when you were taken ill.

James I think Marigold realizes what was in my mind, Iris. (*To Marigold*)
It just seemed peculiar that you should *choose* to stay in.

Marigold I don't see what's wrong with an evening at home. You used to
be the one who enjoyed staying in.

James But we're not hermits. There's nothing wrong with spending an
occasional evening in company.

Marigold There's nothing wrong in keeping oneself to oneself. At least,
there wasn't until the Smedleys moved in.

James Now that's unfair. Time and time again we've had people in for a
drink.

Iris Frequently. What about when Mr Bradshaw used to come over?

James That was while she was in Stevenage.

Iris What about Christmas?

James Christmas. We had one, two, four people over at one point last

Christmas Eve. So let's keep a sense of perspective, Marigold. We may enjoy our privacy but let's hope we are that little bit gregarious. Why, we've been cordiality itself when the occasion has risen. The trouble is that Marigold regards herself as a cut above our neighbours.

Iris She doesn't like them.

Marigold I don't have to like them twenty-four hours a day.

Iris You don't try to like them, Marigold. Take this morning—Thelma popped in to see if I wanted anything from the Stores. (*To James*) She snubbed her.

James I can well believe you.

Marigold But that was the fifth time she popped in. And it was only ten in the morning.

James She was being friendly.

Marigold Before we know where we are, they'll be walking in here without even knocking. We might be eating! You're letting them force themselves on to you!

James Well, there is a precedent in the family, isn't there? No names, no pack drill, but I do remember a certain gentleman paying his attentions in this area. And I personally never took to him. But I don't recollect you recoiling in horror. In fact, I recollect you marrying him. And I'll tell you his name . . .

Iris His name's Harold.

Marigold (*flouncing from her chair and storming across the room*) I wish you'd leave Harold out of it!

James's eyes are still on the chair she has vacated. With Iris's help he moves the chair to another part of the room. They step back and examine the effect

Iris Now that does make a difference!

James What do you think, Marigold?

Marigold (*sulking*) What do I think about what?

James A clear area of floor space. An uncluttered effect. I don't know what you think but I think it does make a difference.

Marigold If the Smedleys put their furniture on the roof you'd think it was clever.

Iris That'll do, Marigold.

James Very humorous, I'm sure. (*He goes over to an occasional table which he is about to move*)

Marigold Don't touch that!

Iris Your father's only carrying out an experiment.

Marigold Then he can experiment with his own furniture. That's my own table that I bought in Stevenage, and I'm not having it moved because it's not where the Smedleys have their table.

James Do you know what you are, Marigold? I don't like to say this in front of your mother and I don't know whether it's attributable to your way of life in Stevenage or what. But I'm beginning to take the view that you're a snob.

Marigold I'm not a snob!

James I'll go further. A stuck-up madam.

James picks up the occasional table and moves it across the room

Marigold He's moved my table!

James I have moved it across my room!

Marigold (*going to the table*) He'd no right to touch it!

James I think I'm allowed to decide on the distribution of furniture in my own home.

Marigold puts the table back where it was. They stare defiantly at each other for some moments. James moves towards the table, but Marigold sits on it

   Marigold, put that table back to where I apportioned it! Marigold, get off your arse and get cracking!

Iris There's no need for that language!

James She'll do as she's told or I'll do it for her!

Marigold Mother, it's my table!

James starts forward and attempts to tip Marigold off the table. A tug-o'-war takes place between the two of them with Iris attempting to intervene

   Smedley enters and takes in the scene

James, with a final tug, is left holding the drawer while Marigold holds the table. The contents of the drawer spill out on the floor

Smedley Whoops-a-daisy!

James and Iris try to look as if nothing has been happening

   Marigold flounces off to her bedroom

   (*Watching her go*) Whoops-Eh-Day-Zee!

James (*holding up the drawer*) We were looking for the Beecham's Powders. For Marigold's migraine.

Smedley I got that. A quick rub down with the *Sporting Life* and seconds out. Come on, then—get stuck in.

Iris We were discussing family matters. (*She picks up the oddments from the floor and replaces them in the drawer*)

Smedley Oh dear, oh doctor, I'm not serious! You don't think I want a ringside seat. You carry on. I'll go tell Thelma. She'll be highly relieved.

James Relieved?

Smedley She thinks you've got the needle. Going off like that. You didn't overstay your welcome, did you?

James (*exchanging a mystified glance with Iris*) We understood you merely asked us to pop in for a drink.

Smedley A drink, yes. You had that all right. A drink. One titchy little gin and ton—and you left half yours, Iris. Thelma thought you'd taken the dead needle. Because of that exploding cigarette.

James Not in the least.

Iris (*replacing the drawer in the table*) We were just saying, we had a very pleasant evening.

Smedley I saw you were when I walked in.

James That was a little family discussion.

Smedley You were having a right ruck, the three of you, weren't you? You've put me in the picture now. You started this barney before you came over to our place, didn't you? You were having a go. Oh, my Christ, Iris says, we've got to go and have drinks with Ken and Thelma. Screw that, says Marigold. We'll make it short and sweet then, Jimmy says, and I'll have a word with you when we get back. I've got it now. A family discussion, that's a new one for it. Sling the table at you, did she?

James Marigold had a migraine and we were . . .

Smedley You ought to see what Thelma slings at me. (*To Iris, indicating his head*) Feel that. Go on, feel it. She did that with a cut-glass vase. (*He takes Iris's hand to guide it to his head*) And that was during a little family discussion. I'd lost seventy nicker at poker. You have got soft hands. "The hands that wash dishes can be soft as your face." They're as soft as a she-mouse's belly, these.

Iris I wear latex gloves.

Smedley Hello, she's smiling! She's smiling, Jimmy! Now's your chance. Kiss and make up.

James I think we can take that as read, Ken.

Smedley Not too proud, are we? Go on. Give her a big french kiss.

Embarrassed, James gives Iris a peck on the cheek

Don't overdo it! Friends again. Now we can carry on where we left off.

Iris Where we left off?

Smedley Having a drink, weren't we? And there's me and Thelma sitting at home with nothing to say. You're stuck in here. There's nothing on telly, I can assure you of that. The night is young. Let's enjoy ourselves.

James We were intending an early night.

Smedley Intending an early night? What for? You dirty old man. (*Guiding Iris towards the door*) Come on, sweetie, you roust out Thelma. Tell her to fetch a drink across. We'll have a real good evening of it!

Heedless of Iris's protestations, Smedley bundles her out into the hall and closes the door on her

Smedley, rubbing his hands, turns back to James

Get the cards out, Jim!

James Can I offer *you* a glass of something, Ken?

Smedley What's on the tariff?

James (*taking a bottle from the sideboard*) I do have a light medium sherry.

Smedley You're having one yourself?

James (*producing two glasses*) Whoops-a-daisy, Ken!

Smedley What about rowing Marigold in?

James I don't think so, Ken. She really has retired to bed.

James gives Smedley a drink which he tosses back

Smedley She's not feeling too well?

James It's nothing to worry about.
Smedley Time of the month?
James Just a little off-colour.
Smedley That's all right, then. So long as it's nothing serious. Nothing physical. Nothing—surgical.
James (*withdrawing momentarily into his shell*) Good heavens, no, Mr Smedley!
Smedley Ken.
James Ken.
Smedley Jimmy.
James (*relaxing again*) No, no, no, no, no. It's simply that Marigold has always been highly strung.
Smedley Yes, I cottoned on to that.

James, wishing to drop the subject, flashes Smedley an embarrassed smile. Smedley beams back—and waits

James May I fill your glass, Ken?
Smedley I shan't say no—if you're having one yourself.

James has to knock back his own untouched drink and pour out more. James pours. They drink

She never mentions her husband, does she? She doesn't talk about him?
James No.
Smedley Funny, that. Take my sister-in-law—Thelma's sister—she never stops rucking about her old man. Three kids he left her with. Seven, five and one in the oven. Goes off to work one morning: clean shirt, best tie, new pair of shoes. Worked in an abattoir! She knew something was wrong. Never set eyes on him again.
James No!
Smedley From that day to this. Never had a penny-piece out of him. Untraceable.
James Surely the police . . . ?
Smedley She's been to the police. The police. The County Court. The Benevolent Association of Slaughter-men. They sent her to the Citizens' Advice Bureau. They couldn't do anything.
James Absolutely disgraceful.
Smedley But I imagine Marigold's case was entirely different.
James Harold—I'm referring to Marigold's husband now—was—is a chartered accountant.
Smedley Chartered, eh? Then you'll have tabs on him.
James He lives in Stevenage.
Smedley He doesn't grumble about paying his whack?
James I'm afraid he doesn't have to. Marigold left *him*.
Smedley She's very fortunate there were no children by the marriage.
James Thank heaven for small mercies.
Smedley There's nothing wrong with her in that direction, Jimmy?
James Which direction would that be, Ken?

Smedley I was just wondering about the cause of her nervous disability. I was wondering if that was a clue to the break-up of her marriage?

James I'm afraid I don't quite follow.

Smedley (*pouring them both a drink*) Well then, how can I circumnavigate the obvious? The reason why she never joined the pudding club? She's not incapable?

James My goodness, no!

Smedley Perhaps it was him that couldn't manage it?

James Harold?

Smedley The chartered accountant. Couldn't give her what-for. Rumpo.

Smedley waits for a response from James, but there is not one forthcoming

Have I gone too far?

James Of course not, Ken.

Smedley I haven't offended you?

James Not in the least.

Smedley But you'd rather not talk about it.

James We try to keep off the subject.

Smedley Put Queen's Park Rangers down to win away next week. Make them a banker. They're an odds on certainty. I've had a bet with a geezer and given him a goal start.

James I'm afraid you're grasping the wrong end of the stick.

Smedley You put the Villa in with a chance then, do you?

James What would you say of a man who . . .

Smedley This is Harold, is it?

James Yes.

Smedley I'm with you.

James Harold is a man of certain habits.

Smedley Aye-aye?

James What I'm getting at is that I wouldn't like you to think the fault was on my daughter's side.

Smedley Six of one and half-a-dozen of the other. It usually is.

James Not in this instance. Marigold was entirely blameless for the break-up of her marriage.

Smedley It does take two to make a quarrel, Jim.

James Not in this instance.

Smedley It was because of his certain habits, then?

James Entirely.

Smedley Then I believe you, Jim.

James You're a man of the world, Ken. I wonder if you could give us some advice.

Smedley Naturally, Jim.

James knocks back his sherry, then takes a document from his bureau

James This is a legal document

Smedley There's nobody trying to do you, is there?

James This is Marigold's divorce petition. She's—er—doing him. May I read it to you?

Smedley What are friends for?

James (*reading*) "Statement of Mrs Marigold Lydia Barker, now residing at Redroofs, The Crescent, Hanley Green, in the County of . . ."

Smedley Skip the codswallop, Jim.

James ". . . and so on and so on. Married Harold Makepeace Barker, and so on and so on—very happy until we returned from Majorca, when I began to observe that my husband was a man of certain tendencies." Certain habits, that is. "We had had frequent sexual intercourse during our honeymoon to which I raised no objection, assuming that when we came to settle in Stevenage my husband would calm down. However, he did not calm down. He continued to demand sexual relations at frequent intervals, sometimes popping home from the office during the day in order to gratify his wishes. On one occasion he demanded his conjugal rights while I was slicing bread. I refused, as the toaster was on and it would have become overheated. He said that I was cold and needed waking up, and that in future he would expect me to be a complete wife in every sense of the word. He purchased an alarm clock which he set to go off at three-hourly intervals during the night, and as I awoke he would demand sexual relations."

Smedley Whoops-a-daisy! Ting-a-ling-a-ling!

James Every three hours. As regular as clockwork. "After six months I went to see our doctor who advised me to move to another bedroom. My husband was amenable to this on condition that when the alarm clock rang I should get up and proceed to the master bedroom. I was ill with influenza for some time, during which my husband stayed away from work to look after me. During this time he demanded sexual relations five times during the day and at the usual three-hourly intervals at night. To the best of my knowledge he has not been unfaithful to me." And so on and so on and so on.

Smedley has been finding it hard to contain his laughter. He waits some moments for James to continue

Smedley Isn't there any more of it?

James I've given you the main area of contention. What's your opinion?

Smedley Over-indulgence, Jimmy. If it was me that was required to give evidence, I'd say there stands a man who is too fond of a good thing.

James I was thinking more in terms of Marigold's character.

Smedley Not a stain upon it.

James I wish I could believe you.

Smedley But what about the other side of it? What's Harold got on her?

James Marigold's behaviour has been exemplary.

Smedley Are you telling me she's not been getting it?

James Since Marigold returned home she has rarely been outside the house.

Smedley But who's been *inside* it? Which Mr Sly-Boots has got his feet under the table?

James Marigold has had no gentleman callers. She is, in name, a married woman.

Smedley Can you swear that under oath?

James I can give my word on it.

Smedley Just supposing I was Harold's counsel. Mr Wormald, I say, and you're standing in the dock. Mr Wormald, you may recall the month of August as being sweltering hot. On the nights when you and your good lady nipped off out for a cooling drink, was your daughter alone in the house?

James Both Mrs Wormald and myself are strict teetotallers.

Smedley (*reprimandingly, indicating James's glass*) Jimmy!

James (*beginning to enjoy the game*) We are not averse to an odd sherry at home with a friend.

Smedley Now we're getting warmer. Were there constant callers at your home?

James I think I can honestly say that we have tried to keep ourselves to ourselves.

Smedley Mr Wormald, are you trying to tell the court that nothing in trousers has been inside your home?

James We did receive a Jehovah's Witness on two consecutive Sundays.

Smedley I think we can safely exclude gentlemen of the cloth? No-one else? Mr Wormald?

James Our neighbours, Mr and Mrs Smedley.

Smedley I know them both personally, me lud, and can vouchsafe for their honesty. Anyone else, Mr Wormald?

James No-one else.

Smedley Then I put it to you that the young lady in question can walk out of this court without a word said against her! Case dismissed, etc.

James Hear-hear! (*Pause*) There is one thing, Ken.

Smedley Jimmy, you've been withholding evidence.

James It's difficult to talk about it.

Smedley When you're taking counsel's opinion?

James It won't go further than these four walls?

Smedley gives him a sorrowful, pitying look

Shortly after Marigold came back to us she was taken very ill.

Smedley Rushed to hospital?

James No, no, no. We managed to keep it to ourselves.

Smedley She tried to get rid of it did she?

James Oh, no, the illness was of her own devising.

Smedley Oh. She had to do away with herself.

James Precisely. She had recourse to take some pills.

Smedley You hadn't been knocking her about, Jimmy?

James Good gracious, no! She seemed completely happy. Totally without reason, that's what we couldn't understand. It wasn't serious at the time, but . . .

Smedley You were worried about a scandal?

James Naturally.

Smedley And you think it might come up?

James In court. In Harold's evidence. He might put forward as argument that Marigold is unstable.

Smedley He knows about it, then?

James Well, not to our knowledge.

Smedley Who does?

James Iris and myself. Marigold, of course. Our family doctor.

Smedley He's covered by your Hippocratic oath. Who else?

James Not a soul in the world—excluding yourself.

Smedley You're safe with me. You've got nothing to worry about.

James Are you positive?

Smedley Absolutely positive. (*Filling both their glasses*) And I think that calls for a celebration drink.

James (*relaxing*) Kenneth . . .

Smedley Ken . . .

James You have taken a great weight from my mind.

Smedley Skol!

James Bottoms up!

Smedley But fair's fair, Jim, you've got to see Harold's side of it.

James I've no particular wish to hear that particular person's name mentioned again.

Smedley (*nudging James*) Every three hours—ting-a-ling-a-ling!

James (*allowing himself a self-conscious smirk*) I suppose, when you put it like that . . .

Smedley Come on, Jimmy! Admit the funny side to it. Brrrr-brrrr. Brrrr-brrrr. Whoops-a-daisy! Off we go again!

James I suppose we might smile at it in the fullness of time. But we are her parents—we do have to consider Marigold's position.

Smedley Whoops-a-daisy! You've cracked one there, Jim! Marigold's position! You're a bit of a sly one, aren't you?

James (*attempting the man-of-the-world*) Ting-a-ling-a-ling?

They both laugh

Smedley Here! Here! I've got one for you, Jim. Do you think he introduced her as his time-piece? Time-piece? Got it, Jim?

James (*allowing himself a mild snigger and holding up the sherry bottle*) Care for another sherry, Ken?

Smedley (*holding out his glass*) Speaking of sherry: this geezer out with this débutante. You know, chap's night away from the missus. Anyway, he's going to get a couple of lamb chops inside her and all back to her place. So. He offers a little pre-dinner snifter. He says, "What will you have, my dear?" He says, "Will you have port or sherry?" So this deb says, I can't do the accent, "I'll have sherry." She says, "When I drink sherry it does wonderful things to me, does sherry." She says, "'Cause when I drink sherry I imagine I'm lying naked—starkers—on a beautiful sun-drenched beach . . ."

James Very good. Whoops-a-daisy, Ken!

Smedley I haven't finished yet, Jim. She says, "When I drink sherry I imagine myself on these wonderful sands. Naked." And she's got some bristols, Jim. "And", she says, "when I drink sherry I imagine this tall, handsome bronzed Greek hero striding out of the sea." And he's as naked as the day he was born, Jim. "And," she says, "he's got this beautiful big shell in his hands and it's full of these tiny, beautiful pink pearls." She says, "And he stands over me and he pours these tiny pearls all down over me—and they go twinkle-twinkle all down over my beautiful naked body!" She says, "That's what happens when I drink sherry. When I drink port," she says ...

They are both doubled up with laughter

James Go on! Go on!
Smedley "When I drink port," she says, "I fart!"

The front door slams, but James does not notice

It's cabaret time!

Iris enters with Thelma, who is carrying a bottle of whisky and a bottle of gin

James, slightly tipsy, continues to giggle. Iris looks at him, slightly disapproving

(*To Thelma*) Hello, Doris!
James Who's Doris?
Smedley Doris Karloff!
Thelma (*to Iris, proudly*) He's been telling his jokes to him.
Iris We could hear you laughing right up the garden path.
James (*pouring a glass of sherry for Iris*) A glass of sherry to make you merry!

Iris accepts the glass with ill-grace and stands hugging it, not drinking

Iris I'm sure I don't know what they must be thinking at Mon Repos.
Thelma You know what men are when they're left together.
James I think we're entitled to a little merry-making in the confines of our own home. Mon Repos or no Mon Repos. A glass of sherry for you, Mrs Smedley?
Smedley For Gawd's sake don't give her a glass of port!

James goes off into peals of laughter

The hall door opens and Marigold, attracted by the noise, peers round it. She is wearing a dressing-gown

Smedley catches sight of her

Come in, sweetie!

Marigold quickly disappears again

Iris flashes James a reproving glance

Iris Marigold hasn't been feeling at all well.

James (*pouring a glass of sherry*) I've already explained to Ken. (*To Thelma*) Our daughter is a little highly-strung.
Smedley She just needs taking out of herself.
Thelma She doesn't need to be shy of us, Iris. Just so long as she takes us as she finds us.
Smedley She's all right, is Marigold. She's a bit reserved, that's all.

Smedley catches sight of James, who is moving carefully towards Thelma with the brimming glass of sherry. Smedley continues without pause

Get with it, Jimmy! (*Taking the glass from him*) You won't get the girls into the party spirit on South African sherry!
Thelma (*moving to the sideboard with her bottles*) Where do you keep your tumblers, Iris?

Iris is too busy restraining Smedley from taking her glass away. Smedley wrests the glass from her and turns his attention to Thelma

Smedley Use your bloody eyes, Thelma! They're in the right-hand cupboard, staring at you!
James (*crossing to help Thelma*) Allow me!
Iris I'm all right with this, thank you.
Smedley We know you're all right, sweetie. It's what you're drinking we're concerned with. We can't have a party without Marigold. Come on. Iris, get your Marigold at it!
James I rather fear that Marigold *has* retired for the night.
Iris She's always shy when we have company.
Smedley I'll bet *I* can get her at it. (*He opens the hall door and calls loudly*) Goodnight, Jimmy! Goodnight, Iris!

Smedley slams the door. Then, dragging Thelma, he crouches in hiding behind the door

After a moment, Marigold appears, still in her dressing-gown

Marigold Really! Some people!
Smedley (*revealing himself*) Whoops-a-daisy! I said I'd get her at it! Come in, Marigold. It's party night!
Thelma Are we keeping you awake, sweetie?

Smedley closes the hall door

Marigold (*forcing a smile*) Not at all, Mrs Smedley. I couldn't sleep, anyway. I just came in for an aspirin but it doesn't . . .

Marigold turns to go back to her bedroom, but Smedley is firmly planted in front of the hall door

Smedley You don't want aspirins. Look at me—never had an aspirin in my life.
Thelma You don't suffer with headaches.
Smedley She doesn't want aspirins.
Thelma I know she doesn't want aspirins.

Smedley I know what Marigold wants. Something to put her back on her feet. She wants a brandy.
Thelma She wants something for her headache!
Smedley A Jack-o-Dandy!
Thelma She doesn't want brandy!

They both study Marigold who, still wearing her dressing-gown, is embarrassed by their attentions. She pulls the collar of her dressing-gown around her throat

She's caught a chill, that's what she's caught, bless her.
Smedley I know what *she* wants.
Thelma I know what she *wants*.

Thelma and Smedley move off together: Thelma to the kitchen and Smedley to the sideboard

Thelma snatches up her handbag en route, and exits

Smedley begins searching through the sideboard cupboards

James Take a pew, Marigold.
Marigold (*appealing to her mother*) I'd much rather go back to bed.
Iris Marigold would be better off in bed.
Smedley Park your bottom!

Marigold looks weakly from James to Iris and then sits on the sofa. Smedley goes to her with a stiff whisky

Thelma enters with a glass of water

(*Giving her the Scotch*) Drink this.
Thelma (*popping a tablet into the glass and handing it to her*) Drink that.
Smedley (*to James*) Straight Scotch—you're out of brandy.
Thelma (*to Iris*) Pheno-Fizzies—much better than aspirins.

The four of them cluster round Marigold, who is clutching a glass in either hand

James Drink it down, Marigold. It'll do you good.
Iris Drink it, Marigold. You'll feel a lot better.

Marigold is forced to sip first at one glass and then at the other, coughing over the whisky. Smedley and Thelma smile approvingly

Smedley No heel-taps.
Thelma Knock it straight back.

As Marigold sips unhappily from both glasses, Thelma glances round the room

I see now what it is that they've done.
Smedley What's that, Thelma?
Thelma They've moved this relaxer lounge from there to here.
Smedley (*to James, proudly*) She doesn't miss much!
Thelma Now I call that a one hundred per cent improvement.
  C

James We were trying for an uncluttered effect. A clear area of floor space.
Thelma (*nodding*) More free and easy.
Smedley Just move that table from there to there, Thelma.

Marigold watches in horror as Thelma crosses to pick up the occasional table

Marigold Mrs Smedley!

Thelma turns, smiling

We like it where it is now.

Thelma picks up the table

We prefer it where it is!

Smedley points to where he wants the table. Thelma moves it. Smedley beams, inviting general approbation

Thelma One hundred per cent improvement.
James (*giving Marigold an I-told-you-so look*) Quite right, Thelma. It really does make a difference.

Smedley, encouraged, picks up one end of the settee—regardless of the fact that Marigold is sitting on it—and swings it round into the centre of the room. Marigold squirms uneasily

Smedley Sit tight, sweetie!

Smedley again beams round, inviting comment

James Bravo, Ken!
Thelma Princess Margaret has hers like that.
Iris It does look more gregarious.
Thelma More free and easy.
Smedley And it brings the invalid into the party. (*He gives Marigold a wink*) Happy there, sweetie?
Marigold Thank you.
Smedley Cheer up, it may never happen!
Marigold I'm quite happy. Really I am.
Smedley Give us a smile then! Show us your dimples!

Marigold manages a tight smile

Whoops-a-daisy!
Iris She's always shy in company.
Marigold Mother, I'm quite happy!
James You don't look it. I'd say you were being downright unsociable.
Marigold I'm quite happy. I've already said so!
James You're hardly the life and soul of the party!
Iris She's always been quiet in company.
Marigold I didn't know we were having a party.
James We're indulging in social intercourse.

Iris is shocked

What else would you call it?

During the above exchange between James and Marigold, Smedley furiously attempts to attract Thelma's attention. He at last succeeds and indicates that she should replenish the glasses. Thelma trots dutifully round with the whisky bottle. Smedley turns his own attentions to the role of peacemaker

Smedley It's cheer-up-Marigold night. Because Marigold's feeling a bit mizzy. Aren't you, sweetie? And we all have our off-days. (*To Iris*) Don't we, sweetie?

Both Iris and Marigold are thankful that the row has been averted and smile gratefully

I know what we're going to do! We're all going to do our best to get Marigold at it!

James (*slightly appeased*) You'll find that you've set yourself a difficult task

Smedley Don't be like that, Jimmy! She's easy! She's smiling already. Look at her little face! She's going! She's cracking.

Marigold's smile broadens

I'll tell you what we'll do. We'll play the Joke Game.

Thelma Oh, I like that.

Smedley Do you know how to play, Jimmy? Everybody tells a joke, in turn. But nobody's got to laugh. Everyone who laughs—ten p. in the kitty. Are you with me?

Thelma You mustn't laugh, you see. If you *do* laugh, you pay up.

Smedley Right. Who's going to start us off? Iris?

Iris I'm afraid I don't know any jokes.

James Iris is hardly the *raconteur* of the family.

Smedley Get away with you. Come on, Iris. You can make it a bit near the knuckle if you like—we're all broadminded.

Iris Very well, then. There were three crows on a post.

James Oh, really Iris. As old as the hills.

Thelma No, let her tell it.

Iris There were three crows on a post. I shot one—how many were left? Somebody's got to say "two".

Smedley All right, I'll buy it. Two.

Iris No, because when I shot the first one the other two flew away.

Silence

So there were none left.

Dead silence

Smedley (*heavily*) Yes. Well. Nobody laughed so nobody pays out. You've all got the hang of it.

Iris I told you I couldn't tell stories.

Thelma Why don't we play it the other way?

Smedley What—like we used to at the Conservative Club?

Thelma It's a scream that way.

Smedley That's it. Right. New rules. Everybody tells a joke in turn—right? Same as before. But. Everybody's got to laugh. Doesn't matter how corny the joke is—doesn't matter if you've heard it ten times before—if you don't laugh you put ten p. in the kitty. Got it?

James I'm afraid I don't quite follow.

Smedley How can I explain? Tell you what—you tell us a joke, Jimmy.

James A joke, a joke, a joke . . .

Smedley Any joke. Doesn't matter if it's terrible.

James Let me see, what was the one that young apprentice told me? What is it that's purple, grows on a tree . . .

Iris An electric plum.

Smedley Let him tell it!

Iris He told me it last week.

Smedley You're missing the point, Iris. Let him finish.

James What is it that's purple, grows on a tree and makes a low humming noise?

Smedley We can't imagine, Jim! What is it that's purple, grows on a tree and makes a low humming noise?

James An electric plum.

Smedley and Thelma immediately go off into gales of laughter. Iris and Marigold do not laugh. Smedley jabs his finger at them

Smedley Ten p. in! Ten p. in!

Marigold But we knew it.

Smedley That's the point! You've got to pee yourself whether you know it or not. Ten p. in the kitty. And you, Jimmy.

James But I told the joke.

Smedley Doesn't matter.

James Oh, I see! Jolly good! Excellent! What an excellent party game.

Thelma (*giving Marigold another drink*) Marigold's turn.

Marigold I'll tell you my limerick.

Smedley Hello!

Marigold (*knocking back her Scotch*) There was a young lady from Kent, who said that she knew what it meant, when men asked her to dine, gave her cocktails and wine—she knew what it meant but she went.

They all roar with rather forced laughter

Smedley Quickie! A little quickie! Did you hear about the geezer who offered the society bird a Scotch and sofa?

Still giggling at the last joke, they all shake their heads

She reclined!

Their laughter is now infectious and unforced

And what about the lady masseur who got the sack for rubbing a customer up the wrong way? I like it, I like it, I like it! You're on, Thelma!

Thelma (*through her laughter*) What about the honeymoon couple?

Smedley (*also hysterical*) The honeymoon couple!

Thelma On honeymoon! So the blushing bride says to her husband—in bed—first night—she says, "Darling will you love me always?" "Of course I will, sweetie," he says. "Which way would you like to try first?"

They are all five hysterical, though the Wormalds are hardly aware what they are laughing at

Smedley Another quickie! Just a quickie! Wait a minute! I've got one! It's—it's . . . Listen to this! The shortest joke in the world! Ready? Stop laughing! Are you all ready?

They all attempt to control their laughter

Here we go then! Shortest joke in the world! Ting-a-ling-a-ling! Ting-a-ling-a-ling!

Thelma is immediately hysterical, although she does not know why. Iris and Marigold, following the rules of the game, laugh too. James is at first doubtful, but then joins in

Ting-a-ling-a-ling!

James rushes out of the room and comes back with a ringing alarm clock

Marigold and Iris, realizing what they have been laughing at, stop short

James Ten p. in!

Iris, at this, begins to laugh again. James nudges Marigold and, more uncertain than the others, she laughs, too. The Smedleys have not stopped laughing, and soon all five are beside themselves, as—

the CURTAIN *falls*

ACT II

Scene 1

The same. The following morning

Iris sits at the breakfast table on the patio, plainly nursing a hangover—the first one she has ever had. From one of the bedrooms comes the sound of a female voice raised in song—someone feels better than Iris does, and it makes her wince. A vacuum-cleaner flex leads into the living-room from one of the bedrooms. After a moment Thelma—it is she who is singing—comes into the living-room, unplugs the flex, and goes off again. Marigold, who has an even worse hangover than Iris, comes out of the kitchen and crosses to the patio carrying two glasses of Alka-Seltzer which she and Iris drink

Iris (*wrinkling her nose*) Bubbles up my nose.

Marigold It'll do us both good.

Iris Would you like some breakfast now, Marigold?

Marigold I couldn't, Mother. I never want to eat again.

Iris How many times have you used the bathroom?

Marigold Quite often.

Iris I haven't used it very often. I used it when I got up and I used it again after I had a piece of dry toast.

Marigold I've used it frequently.

Iris You always did have a weak tummy, even when you were a baby.

Marigold Have you tried closing your eyes? It's awful.

Iris (*closing her eyes*) Why did you want to suggest a silly thing like that?

Marigold I wasn't sure if it was just me.

Iris It is a general effect. Your father had it at three o'clock this morning.

Marigold I'm surprised he was able to eat any breakfast.

Iris Ah, well he had the good sense to use the bathroom in the early hours. Your father was very wise in that respect. We let it settle and so we're the victims. We'd know better if it happened again.

Marigold It isn't going to happen again.

Iris I wasn't suggesting that it was, Marigold. (*Pause*) You know you were dancing with Mr Smedley, don't you?

Marigold I wasn't the only one. Father was dancing with Mrs Smedley. He was enjoying it. I didn't want to dance with Mr Smedley. He literally dragged me on to my feet. There's quite a distinct bruise on my shoulder.

Iris It was the *way* you were dancing with him, Marigold.

Marigold I couldn't help it. He told me it was a cha-cha-cha.

Iris I knew it was a rumba from the moment he put the record on. I'm only glad we remembered to draw the curtains. I should hate to wonder what a casual passer-by might have thought.

Marigold You were dancing as well, Mother.

Iris I was performing the regulation steps taught to me by the Corona School of Dancing as a girl.

Marigold Yes, but by yourself.

Iris I couldn't come to much harm dancing by myself.

Marigold I thought it was in very bad taste.

Iris The whole evening was in bad taste, Marigold. Do you think another Alka-Seltzer would do any good?

Marigold I'm going to use the bathroom before I try anything else.

Iris I'm not too sure that it wouldn't be best to bring everything up and then make a fresh start on the day.

Marigold Mother!

Iris It's no use being evasive about these things. And as for the Smedleys, we must make it quite clear to them that that isn't the kind of evening we're used to enjoying.

Marigold We must make it quite clear to them that it isn't going to happen again.

Thelma enters the living-room from the hall

Iris Yes, dear.

Marigold When I said that last night, *you* said I was being anti-social.

Iris Yes, well. You can have too much of a good thing.

Thelma picks up several long-playing records which are strewn about the room and calls out to Iris

Thelma *Two Moods of Winifred Atwell*. Is that yours or ours?

Iris That's yours.

Thelma John Hanson sings *The Student Prince?*

Marigold Ours.

Thelma (*moving out to the patio*) I've finished the bedrooms. All done and dusted. I'll just run round your toilet and then everything's finished.

Iris Thank you. I don't know what we'd have done without you.

Thelma What are neighbours for? If you're feeling a bit better by lunch time I usually make a chopped egg mayonnaise Saturdays. You're most welcome to come over.

Iris It's very kind of you to offer but I don't think we will.

Thelma You don't want to knock yourself out cooking. You're most welcome, you know. (*To Marigold*) Make her come.

Marigold It's very kind of you to offer but I don't think we will.

Thelma You'd be most welcome.

Thelma goes into the living-room. Iris and Marigold exchange triumphant smiles at the stand they have made. Thelma returns

It must be hot out there in October.

Iris Where?

Thelma The Costa del Sol.

Iris and Marigold react with horror at a simultaneous recollection

You'd forgotten, hadn't you?

Iris (*forcing a smile*) How could we forget? We arranged to share a villa.

Thelma Ken wouldn't let me get to sleep for talking about it. Fancy you forgetting—you must have had a skinful. It was the second fortnight in October we said?

Iris That was when we said.

Thelma He'll surprise you on holiday, will Ken. It takes him right out of himself. You'll have to get yourself a bikini, he said to me in bed. Them Spaniards enjoy a bit of bare flesh. (*To Marigold*) Do you show any off?

Marigold Any what?

Thelma Flesh?

Marigold shakes her head

That's just what I told Ken. We know who it is who can't keep his hands off flesh. I'm looking forward to it.

Thelma goes back into the living-room and continues tidying up. Iris and Marigold stare at each other and as Thelma is still within earshot, enter into a soundless but elaborately mouthed heated conversation

James enters from the hall. He has been shopping and carries two paper bags from a men's store.

James Good morning, Thelma! (*Calling to Iris*) Good morning, sweetie! Still feeling dodgy?

Thelma She's perking up a bit. Did you get the brochures?

James Brochures?

Marigold (*entering from the patio*) The Costa del Sol, Father. You invited Mr and Mrs Smedley to come with us to the Costa del Sol.

James had also forgotten. As the memory returns he is, at first, unsure whether or not to regret the invitation. He looks from Marigold, who is frowning, to Thelma, who is beaming

Thelma He's a devil on holiday is Ken! Once he lets himself go. I *am* looking forward to it!

James (*making up his mind*) So am I!

Thelma, having finished tidying the room, sweeps off into the kitchen

Do you know, the traffic in town gets worse every week!

Marigold We can't take them with us, Father!

Iris (*entering from the patio*) Do you think it's wise, James?

James Perk up, Iris. The hand of friendship has been extended. We can hardly retract it now.

Marigold What about our neighbours on the Costa del Sol? Supposing the Phillipses are there again this year? In the Villa Espagnol?

Iris What about the Teesdales in the Villa Ole?

James The Teesdales and the Phillipses are our neighbours for one single fortnight. The Smedleys are our neighbours—and our friends—for fifty-two weeks in the year.

Iris I hadn't considered it like that, James.

James What is more, the Teesdales *and* the Phillipses are utterly devoid of any *joie de vivre*.

Iris Your father is right there, Marigold.

Marigold Mother!

Iris They are old stick-in-the-muds, you do have to admit that.

James (*loftily*) I have every intention, this year, of rowing both the Teesdales and the Phillipses out. (*He unwraps one of his parcels*)

Marigold (*incredulously*) Why? Because the Smedleys have wormed their way in?

Iris Oh, Marigold, don't say wormed!

Marigold And you've let them do it! You're allowing yourself to be dominated.

James Nonsense.

Iris Now that is nonsense, Marigold.

James finishes unwrapping the parcel and holds up a blazer which boasts a hideous gold wire Royal Army Pay Corps badge

Let's see it on.

Marigold I'm not going to the Costa del Sol with the Smedleys and if you don't tell them I shall.

James, ignoring Marigold, puts on the blazer. Iris admires it

Iris That's nice.

Marigold I'm not going, Father.

James, still ignoring her, takes a corduroy cap from his other bag

Iris Now that *is* nice.

Marigold I'm not, Father.

James puts on his cap and now looks exactly like Smedley

Iris (*unconsciously imitating Thelma*) And that's what I call a one hundred per cent improvement.

Marigold Father! I'm not.

James You're asking for a crack across the arse, young lady.

Marigold I'm not going on holiday with the Smedleys and that's final!

James grabs her wrist, drags her towards him, and with his free hand gives her a resounding smack across her buttocks

James And that's bloody well final!

Marigold, stung with pain and suffering embarrassment and indignity, rubs her bottom. She stares at James incredulously. James comes to his senses immediately, realizes what he has done and is deeply ashamed. He takes off the corduroy cap, and looks at it in disbelief, then looks at Iris and Marigold

Iris I'm sure your father didn't mean to hit you, Marigold.

James puts the cap down as if expunging himself of some of the blame

Marigold I don't want him to talk to me—ever again.

James Marigold . . .

Iris That wasn't like you, James.

Marigold I don't want to talk to him, or eat with him or even look at him —ever again.

Iris I'm sure he's sorry for what he did.

James Marigold, I know that an apology is of little consequence under the circumstances . . .

James's voice trails off as his eyes meet Marigold's. They hold each other's glance for some moments

Marigold (*incredulously and almost childishly*) You hurt me!

Marigold turns and rushes from the room, slamming the door

James (*attempting to bluff it out*) Though why I'm apologising I do not know. She's been asking for that all week.

Iris (*seeing through the bluff*) Try not to blame yourself, James.

James I do not blame myself.

Iris It's all that drinking we were doing. We're not used to it. It upsets the whole system. It puts you out of sorts.

James (*seizing on the excuse*) Yes, we did rather overdo it. Well, we shall just have to watch our evenings in future.

Iris Not have too many of them.

James Not make a habit of it. (*Taking off the blazer*) Yes, that's easily remedied.

Iris You'll have to have a word with Ken and Thelma, James.

James (*sitting*) I don't see why. Good gracious, I've agreed in principle. We're seeing too much of the Smedleys—granted. We've been too high-spirited—granted. Very well. We are our own masters. We won't see so much of them.

Iris We're going over to them tonight. We've asked them over for Sunday dinner. You've invited Mr Smedley to look over the works. We've agreed to have lunch with them at the Conservative Club—you said we'd make a day of it. And we have asked them to the Costa del Sol. Marigold does have a point. A whole fortnight together.

James I know we invited them—we'll just have to edge our way out of it.

Iris You'll have to have a word with them.

James (*reluctantly*) Very well, Iris. I'll have a word with them. (*He broods for some moments and then suddenly leaps to his feet*) Good heavens, Iris, what am I going to say to them? Why can't people have the good sense to keep themselves to themselves? If it isn't Marigold's divorce it's the Jehovah's Witnesses and if it isn't the Jehovah's Witnesses it's the blessed Smedleys! I didn't ask them to move in next door. I didn't ask them to barge their way in.

Iris I'm sure it's just a matter of having a word with them, James.

James But it's all very embarrassing. What am I supposed to say? Thank you very much for coming round but would you kindly refrain from doing so in the future?

Iris You can't say that, James!

James I can't understand why I should have to say anything. It's the Smedleys who moved in. Why should I be saddled with explanations and excuses and apologies? We've got our own lives to lead and we have a right to lead them.

Iris It's very difficult.

James It's easier said than done.

Smedley enters the patio with a cine-camera

Iris You'll think of something.

James, deep in thought and unaware of what he is doing, picks up the occasional table and crosses to put it back in its original position

James But it's got to be a credible excuse. We don't want to hurt their feelings.

James is still holding the table as he becomes aware of Smedley, who is pointing the cine-camera at him.

Smedley Move about a bit!

James (*awkwardly*) Good morning, Ken.

Smedley Don't talk. Just walk about a bit. Act natural.

James and Iris, embarrassed at being filmed, stand stock-still. James is still holding the table

Nip around the room a bit! Your every action is being recorded for posterity on super eight.

James and Iris exchange a glance and decide to make a stand. They both hold their rigid positions. Smedley is in no way put out

I'll tell you what. You both stand still—I'll practise zooming in.

Smedley, his camera whirring, enters from the patio filming James. He lowers the camera

Japanese job. Battery driven. We'll have some high old jinks with this on the Costa del Sol.

Smedley again raises his camera and this time films the motionless Iris. She glances agitatedly at James

Iris James was going to have a word with you about that.

Smedley (*turning his camera on the motionless James*) Oh, yes?

James Er—yes.

Smedley Oh, yes?

James I'm afraid I'll have to ask you to forgive me for last night, Ken.

Smedley (*lowering his camera*) Oh, yes?

James I'm afraid I got rather carried away by the conviviality of the evening.

Smedley Oh, yes?

James Yes. As Iris tactfully pointed out to me over breakfast this morning, I'm afraid we rather rashly made promises which we won't be able to fulfil. As Iris—tactfully pointed out over—breakfast—this—morning.

Smedley Oh, yes?

James Certain promises which, under examination, I was not in a position to make.

Smedley About the Costa del Sol?

James I'm afraid we shall have to cancel our proposed foursome—for this year at least.

Smedley Oh, yes?

James I'm afraid so.

Smedley We can't come with you?

James (*on firmer ground*) Hardly that, Ken. *We* can't come with *you*.

Iris We're very much afraid we can't.

James No. You see, rather foolishly, having drunk too deep of the grape, I neglected to remember that we had already committed ourselves for our little jaunt this year.

Smedley Oh dear me.

James You see, Iris happens to have a very dear sister . . .

Iris (*catching on*) In Bournemouth.

James Who lives in Bournemouth.

Iris Mabel.

James Mabel. To whom we are both very much attached. What I overlooked last night, and only because of the conviviality of the circumstances, was that we have already committed ourselves, in writing, to spend a week with her.

Iris A fortnight.

James Twelve days to be exact. Friday till Monday.

Smedley So you won't be going to the Costa del Sol?

James Not in this instance.

Iris We won't be able to.

Smedley Pity.

James It's a great pity.

Iris We were looking forward to it.

Smedley, downcast, fiddles with his camera. James and Iris, not knowing what to say, watch him in silence. He looks up, catches their glance and flashes them a brave smile

Smedley Not to worry. We'll survive. (*He goes back to pensively fiddling with his camera*)

James There's no reason why we shouldn't manage it next year, Ken.

Smedley It's Thelma I'm concerned about. She'd set her heart on it. (*Indicating the telephone*) May I?

James nods. Smedley goes over and dials.

(*On the telephone*) Thel? Ken this end. . . . I'm over at Jimmy's. . . . Just a minute, sweetie. (*He puts his hand over the mouthpiece and smiles at Iris*) She's dug her swimming cozzie out of the mothballs. She wants you to nip across and once it over.

Iris gives him an embarrassed smile. He turns back to the telephone

Listen, sweetie, I'm afraid it's bad news. . . . Calm down! Keep your
knickers on! No, there's nothing wrong with Jimmy. . . . Jimmy's fine. . . .
And Iris. (*Again to Iris, his hand over the mouthpiece*) Marigold?

Iris nods

(*Back into the telephone*) Yes, Marigold's on top of the world too.
(*Back to Iris*) She thinks of everybody except herself. (*Back into the telephone*) Hang on a minute, Thel! It's no great tragedy. . . . Well, I'm
trying to tell you, aren't I? I'm trying to break it gently, that's all. Right
then. I'll give you three guesses. What's the worst thing that could possibly happen in the whole world? . . . No, scrub round World War
Three. I mean to you—personally? . . . (*To Iris and James*) Would you
credit it? She's got it first shot! (*Back into the telephone*) I'm afraid so,
darling. It's off. . . . Definitely. . . . There isn't any way of getting round
it, and if you'll give me a minute I'll explain. . . . Don't cry. The problem
is that Iris has got this invalid sister. . . . Thelm. (*To Iris*) You won't
mind me saying that? It makes it easier.

Iris and James shake their heads

Iris Mabel.
Smedley (*back into the telephone*) —this invalid sister Mabel who lives in . . .
James Bournemouth.
Smedley (*into the telephone*) Bournemouth. . . . That's right. You've got
the picture. . . . So there we are. Clobbered. Finito. Al kaputt. . . . That's
my girl. Chin up. Be good. (*He puts down the telephone, flashes James
and Iris a smile, picks up his camera and examines it*)
James Everything—all right?
Smedley Fine. Fine. She's a trouper, isn't she? I'll nip across in a couple of
minutes and give her a gee-up. Not to worry. No harm done.

*Still wearing his brave face, Smedley beams round the room. He spots the
corduroy cap and picks it up. He looks enquiringly at James. James nods*

(*With a feeble attempt at his old ebullience*) Whoops-a-daisy. (*He
frowns*) No, it's funny, but we were really looking forward to being with
you three on the Costa del Sol.
James These things will happen. (*To hide his embarrassment, he toys with
the cine-camera*)
Iris They're all sent to try us.
Smedley Anyway. Alla keef. I'll give her a dirty week-end on the Isle of
Wight.
Iris (*after a pause*) Would anybody care for a cup of instant?
Smedley Not for me, sweetie. I'd better nip across and cheer the old girl
up.

Smedley turns to pick up his camera. James is still toying with it

Are you a dab hand with one of those things?
James (*happy that the subject has been changed*) I'm afraid I never progres-
sed further than a Box Brownie, Ken.

Smedley Borrow it.

James No, no, no . . .

Smedley Go on! Take it. Why not? Take it down to Bournemouth. I'll get the projector out when you get back. We'll have an evening of films together.

Iris That would be something to look forward to.

Smedley I've got one or two tucked away that would make your hair stand on end.

Iris simpers

James (*cautiously*) Yes. We might all have an enjoyable evening to-gether—when we all get back.

Smedley (*fervently*) You're a bloody good sort, Jim!

James Nonsense.

Smedley No, in all seriousness, I mean it, Jim.

James That's—very nice of you to say so, Ken.

Smedley I mean it. You're a bloody good sort.

James I appreciate that.

Smedley I knew it from the moment I walked in this house. Sometimes you look at somebody, first time off, and something clicks.

James (*with a glance at Iris*) I must confess, we rather took to you.

Iris Definitely. From the moment you walked in.

Smedley I've never been one for making friends.

James We've always tended to keep ourselves to ourselves.

Smedley Casual acquaintances, yes. I must have had a million. Chance meetings. In pubs and clubs. We've had some fantastic evenings, Thel and me. I don't have to tell you, you can guess. Just mixing in with couples in clubs. Finding yourself at somebody's table. Fantastic evenings. Couples we've never seen before or since. Total strangers. Do you know, I've made them pee themselves. Irrespective of race colour or creed—clubs, common boozers and the best hotels. One night in Reading we were with a Jewish couple once. They weren't ashamed of it. Bloody good sorts. I even cracked a couple of Yiddish gags. He laughed. He did, he laughed. Of course, they were the mild variety. anyway, he laughed at them. They seemed to take to us. We gave them the phone number. They were going to ring us up. Mine host calls closing time—we never set eyes on the bastards again. And it isn't the Jewish angle because the same thing has happened with true-blue Englishmen. I don't know what it is I do to people.

Smedley stares at James, inviting an answer. James clears his throat, but does not speak. Smedley approaches him aggressively

Do I suffer from B.O. or something?

James (*making a nervous joke*) I'm sure your best friends would tell you about that, Ken!

Smedley Well then what, in God's name, have I done to offend?

James Why—nothing, Ken.

Smedley (*with a sudden change of mood*) Scrub round it, Jimmy.

James I can honestly assure you, Ken, that the arrangements to visit Bournemouth stem from a long-standing agreement.

Smedley Forget it, Jim.

Iris You see, we promised Mabel a long time ago. Before you and Thelma moved in.

Smedley You don't have to make excuses—I *like* you, you silly twats.

James The true fact of the matter is that the Costa del Sol has always been a biennial excursion.

Iris Every other year.

James Yes, one year it's the Costa del Sol. The following year it's Bournemouth.

Iris She's my only sister. She's getting on. We don't see very much of her.

James And we are rather attached.

Smedley, though crestfallen, is smiling sympathetically. James looks at him, wavers, and is lost

It's not as if we've ever been particularly friendly with her.

Iris Not exactly friendly—more attached.

James Exactly.

A pause. Smedley nods

Apart from holidays we never bother with her.

Iris It isn't as if she ever comes to see us.

James She doesn't put *her*self out for us. She isn't a friend in the true sense of the word.

Iris More of a relative.

James You could say that. One can choose one's friends, but one's relatives are thrust upon one. Iris, I think we will go to the Costa del Sol!

Smedley I haven't talked you into it?

James Certainly not!

Smedley (*a smile slowly spreading across his face*) Whoops-a-daisy! (*Picking up his camera*) I'll be snapping you in the altogether on them sun-drenched beaches before you can say Brigitte Bardot.

James With a glass of sherry held aloft!

Smedley Whoops-a-daisy!

James (*putting on his new cap at a jaunty angle*) Olé!

Smedley (*filming James*) We'll have a bit of that!

James performs a clumsy pirouette. Smedley backs out on to the patio to widen his camera angle

(*Gesticulating at Iris*) Get into the picture, sweetie!

Iris (*simpering, as she moves to join James*) What shall I do?

Smedley Give us a lovey-dovey picture. Cuddle up.

James takes Iris in his arms and strikes a silent movie pose

Whoops-EH-DAISEE! Action! Print that! Now dance around a bit. Astair and Rogers stuff.

James and Iris put their arms about each other's waists and go into a shambl-ing jog-trot. Smedley watches them

Hang about a bit. If a job's worth doing . . . (*He puts his camera down on the patio table and moves into the room to the record-player*) We'll have a bit of music on. (*He glances at a record left on the turntable, and switches the player on*) What a *good* tune!

As the record-player warms up the music increases in volume. The record is an L.P. of "The Merry Widow", the track is the Finale to Act 1

It's one of Thelma's favourites is this. (*Suddenly recollecting*) Oh blimey, Thelma! She's probably hanging herself, right this minute, in the bloody loo!

James The Costa del Sol!

Iris She doesn't know we're going!

James Give her a tinkle, Ken.

Smedley Not on your nelly! This calls for personal representation.

James Why don't we all nip over and break the news?

The three of them rush out into the hall and we hear the front door slam

The record-player is still playing

After some moments, Marigold enters

She glances warily around and is pleased to find that she is alone. She moves to the record-player and stands swaying gently to the music. She is smiling contentedly, and then frowns as a thought crosses her mind. She switches the record-player off. She lifts up her dressing-gown and examines her thigh, looking for a bruise where James struck her. Finding the dressing-gown an encumbrance she takes it off. She is wearing a modest slip. She again peers at her thigh and then, having ascertained that she hasn't suffered any lasting scars, loses interest. She turns the record over and switches on the player. With Marigold we listen to the strains of "Love Unspoken" from "The Merry Widow". Marigold hums and sways gently to the song of the male duettist. As the female duettist takes up the song, Marigold, associating herself with the singer, moves around the room to the music

Smedley, who has come back to pick up his camera, appears on the patio unseen by Marigold

As Marigold, lost in a world of her own, drifts around the room in her slip, Smedley picks up his camera and films her. Marigold sees Smedley. Em-barrassed and confused she snatches up her dressing-gown. Smedley, un-invited, walks in

Smedley I suppose you know that you were showing everything you've got?

Marigold If you were a gentleman you wouldn't have stood there looking. (*She stops the record-player*)

Smedley (*indicating the window*) Not only me, sweetie. You were treating half the neighbourhood.

Marigold (*changing the subject*) If you're looking for my parents, I think they've gone out, Mr Smedley.

Smedley Why can't you call me Ken?

Marigold Because I'm not in the habit of calling people by their first names.

Smedley Not even when they've caught you in your underclothes?

Marigold does not reply

Don't you call them by their first names then? I bet you called Harold by his first name.

Marigold Of course I did. I was married to him.

Smedley You didn't like him.

Marigold What's that got to do with it?

Smedley You called him Harold.

Marigold After I'd been introduced to him.

Smedley And then you called him Harold all the time?

Marigold I suppose so—yes.

Smedley Even when you hated him?

Marigold I didn't hate him.

Smedley Not even when *he* caught you in your underclothes?

No reply

When the alarm went off? Ting-a-ling-a-ling? When the balloon went up? I'll bet you didn't call him Harold then? Not when you were having arguments? Were you having an argument about me this morning?

Marigold Who says I was having an argument this morning?

Smedley You were sulking in your room when I came in.

Marigold You don't miss much, do you, Mr Smedley?

Smedley Ken. No, not a lot. I sussed the temperature. And your face is blotchy. Did he swipe you one? He did, didn't he? You wake up, screaming hangovers all over you, Marigold's a bit snappy and crack! Right across the face! Am I right or wrong?

Marigold (*accusingly*) It wasn't the face, it was the—another part.

Smedley So he clocked you one? He's a tartar when his bottle's gone, your old man. Has he marked you for life? Let's have a skeg. (*He grabs at the sleeve of Marigold's dressing-gown and pulls her towards him*)

Marigold Mr Smedley, let me go!

Smedley I'll have him up before the N.S.P.C.C. if there's a bruise on you.

Marigold Please!

Smedley Come on, let's have a look then.

Marigold (*trying to free herself*) Let go of me!

Marigold turns on him with such passionate intensity that Smedley in surprise, releases her

(*as if apologizing for her outburst*) You'll tear my négligé.

Smedley You've spoiled your face with crying. Do you know?

Marigold (*self-pityingly*) There isn't much to spoil.

She turns her back on him. He approaches her from behind, cautiously, and speaks soothingly, as if he were talking to a child

D

Smedley You're a silly girl, Marigold. What are you? A silly girl. If you
screw your face up like that, do you know what'll happen? You'll go like
it. You will, you know. (*Standing close behind her, his hands resting gently
on her shoulders*) You'll go like it.

Marigold does not move

Is it because Jim took his hand to you? I know what you're thinking.
If only Harold was here—*he'd* give him one, right across the chops. I bet
he was a lad, eh? Harold? Do you wish you had him back? Do you?
It's not the end of the world, you know. It's not as bad as all that. Wait
till we're all in our coffins, lying down, then we'll have something to cry
about. No nights out then. No fun. No parties, no jokes, no getting
drunk. (*He slips his arm around her waist and gently massages her back
with his free hand*) We won't have much to live for when we're dead, eh?
I wouldn't be dead for a thousand pounds.

She shivers involuntarily and allows him to draw her closer

(*Quietly*) Whoops-a-daisy, Marigold.

*Marigold turns to him and they kiss passionately. Smedley is taken aback by
her ardour. He stands away from her, breathing heavily. Marigold appears
outwardly calm. She unbuttons her dressing-gown and lets it fall on the floor.
She looks towards the settee but Smedley shakes his head. On impulse, he
crosses to the hall door and opens it*

*Marigold goes through to her bedroom. He follows, closing the hall door.
The room is empty for some moments before James and Iris enter via the
patio. James, in high spirits, bounds into the living-room*

James Fall in the Spanish Brigade! Stand by your ... (*He breaks off,
surprised to find the living-room deserted*)
Iris (*picking up the dressing-gown*) I do wish that girl'd train herself not to
leave things lying about.

Iris goes through to the hall

James He must have gone off to the pub. (*He trails off as he sees the camera,
and picks it up*)

Iris comes back into the room carrying the dressing-gown

Iris Her bedroom door's locked.

*Iris, holding the dressing-gown, and James, holding the camera, look at
each other*

James I assume she's in bed, then.
Iris I assume she is.

*Their glances switch to the objects each other is holding. There is a long
silence*

James Should I knock on the door, do you think?
Iris What would you say? What *could* you say?
James I should think of something, make no doubt of that.

Iris I'm sure you would. (*A pause*) You couldn't smack her again. You've done that once, and it was once too often. She'd walk out. She'd pack her bags and walk out.

James No. I wouldn't raise my hand to her.

Iris Well, then. What?

James quietly closes the hall door

James It's a matter for thought. I should have to think of something. It's a question of whether it would be *right* to interfere?

Iris She is entitled to her own life.

James If she wants to—take to her bed in broad daylight, it's her own affair.

Iris If you should say anything, she might get very upset. And you know how she carries on when she's upset.

James Perhaps we should let the matter be?

Iris That's for you to decide, James.

James You don't think that would be taking a complacent attitude?

Iris She has been tired lately. Peaky. I think the rest might do her good.

James (*using an unconscious Smedleyism*) She's been walking about like a tart in a trance.

Iris She hasn't been sleeping at all well.

James She's been a right old misery-guts.

Iris She gets upset very easily.

James Anyway, to hell with it. It's the modern generation, isn't it? It's how they carry on.

Iris It's the younger end. They don't behave like us.

James There's only one fly in the jam-pot. What the knickers are we going to do when they . . . Well, when she wakes up?

Iris I was thinking of popping into town for a nylon bathroom rug. So it's more than likely I shall be out—if she should wake up.

James (*slipping on his blazer and cap*) There are one or two prezzies I promised myself I forgot to pick up. I might shoot off into town with you. Do you think we've time for a glass of sherry before we move?

Iris Oh, I think so. We could make a little shopping expedition out of it. Stay out for lunch. The Kardomah.

James Or the Dirty Duck. (*He pours the sherry and hands a glass to Iris*) Right then. First today.

Iris Bottoms up.

James Bottoms up.

CURTAIN

SCENE 2

The same. That afternoon

The living-room is as we left it at the end of Scene 1—except that the dressing-gown and camera have been removed. The front door slams, and some moments later, the hall door is pushed cautiously open. Iris, wearing her hat at a jaunty angle, peers in. Iris and James have just returned from their afternoon in town. They have had a couple of drinks, and Iris is rather tipsy. James has a carrier-bag with him

Iris (*peering conspiratorially round the door*), The birds have flown! (*She enters, taking off her coat*) They're not in here either. Would you believe it, she tidied up her bedroom when she finished, and she made the bed. (*Noticing the absence of the dressing-gown*) *And* she's put her dressing-gown away! That's not like her. There must be some hope for Miss Dozy-Drawers yet . . . Eeeeeeeyow!

Iris screams and sits heavily as she catches sight of James. He is standing in the hall doorway with a joke hatchet buried in his head

James Whoops-a-daisy!
Iris Oooooh, Jimmy, it's a good one is that!

James acknowledges Iris's appreciation of his little prank by switching on and off the joke light-up bow-tie which he is wearing

James (*holding up a carrier-bag*) And I've got a million of 'em in my little bag!
Iris I did enjoy that trick you showed the gentleman in that little bar we went in.
James The miserable bastard! It'll be a long long time before I enter the portals of the Tom-Tom Club again.
Iris He nearly jumped out of his skin!
James The snotty-nosed sod! Are you a member, he says? I ask you? Do I look like a bloody member, of the bloody Tom-Tom Club? Would you mind signing the visitors' book, he says, and I'll introduce you.
Iris And then you gave him that pen.
James (*producing a pen from his breast pocket*) The little Atomic Wonder pen! (*He pulls the cap from the pen, which explodes*) That topped the geezer!
Iris (*giggling*) You'll have to try that out on Ken. (*Suddenly serious*) I wonder if they've gone for a walk or something?
James Who?
Iris Him and Marigold. Marigold and Ken.
James And left Thelma all on her ownio? Talk sense! (*Pouring drinks*) I'll

lay odds that Ken shot off home before Thelma noticed he was A.W.O.L. from the family nest.

Iris (*slightly perturbed*) Then where has Marigold gone?

James Out. Thank Christ. Into God's good air.

Iris It isn't like Marigold to go out on her own.

James (*handing Iris a drink*) It's not before bloody time. It'll do her good. Mark my words, sweetie, Marigold will be a different woman from now on.

Iris She even made the bed after . . . When she got up.

James (*sniggering*) I'll bet it needed it!

Iris James Wormald!

James (*stifling his snigger, thinking he has perhaps gone too far*) I think we can safely say our little shopping spree was fully worthwhile.

Iris If you think he has done her good.

James Indubitably. Mission accomplished! Roger and out! Skol!

Iris (*rising to drink the toast*) Bottoms up.

James snatches at opportunity and playfully pinches her bottom

James!

James (*winking his light-up bow-tie on and off*) I'm seriously considering the possibility of giving you one tonight.

Iris (*tipsily coquettish*) Whoops-a-daisy.

James Indeed taking into account the welcome absence of Little Miss Prissy-Pants, I'm seriously considering the possibility of giving you one right now!

James playfully chases Iris around the furniture

Smedley appears on the patio

Smedley Go on, my son!

James and Iris come to a halt, rather sheepishly. Smedley enters the room. His usual bonhomie is rather forced; beneath it he is ill at ease. He too has been drinking

So—the wanderers return.

James switches on his light-up bow-tie. Smedley reacts, but without real enthusiasm

Whoops-a-daisy.

James I've got one for you, Ken. (*He fishes a squeaky cushion from his carrier-bag and blows it up*) One for you, is this. Remember? When I drink sherry I feel golden fingers up my spine, but when I drink port . . . (*He sits on the squeaky cushion*) Who said that!

Smedley (*again without enthusiasm*) Very good.

James (*with a puzzled glance at Iris*) I've got a quickie for you, Ken.

Iris Tell him about the club.

James The club! The bloody Tom-Tom Club! Anyway, we waltz into this drinking club—Iris and me. Big chucker-out comes up . . .

Smedley I know. You told me.

James (*hurt*) It only happened this afternoon.
Smedley (*peering into the hall*) Marigold about?
James She's gone out.

James is puzzled at Smedley's lack of co-operation in the fun. Iris spurs him on

Iris Try him with one of your cigarettes.
James (*smiling again, and producing a packet of cigarettes*) Have a snout.
Smedley It's a joke one.
James Just try one, Ken. Go on.

Smedley puts a cigarette in his mouth. James, with due ceremony, gives him a light. James and Iris wait expectantly. A blue flame shoots out of the trick cigarette. James and Iris await Smedley's approval

Smedley (*as if nothing had happened*) Did she—er—say anything?
James Who?
Smedley Marigold?
James What about?
Smedley Anything?
Iris We haven't had a chance to speak to her. She was out when we got back.
Smedley (*slightly relieved, pointing to the hatchet which is buried in James's head*)That's a good one! It's a cracker, is that!
James (*believing he has assessed Smedley's preoccupation*) Sit down. Ken.

Smedley, nervous, does not move

  Get your arse in that chair, lad!

Smedley sits

  Better, better! Father is about to speak freely in his own home. Subject—recent activities of female offspring.

Smedley glances nervously at Iris

  Relax Ken. Iris is fully conversant with my attitude towards Marigold. Briefly, all I want to say is, I'm grateful to you, Ken.

Smedley is amazed and James is gratified

  What a turn up, eh? It's true, Ken. My daughter was frustrated. Make no mistake about that. Frustrated. Never went out, moped about the house. Frustration. I put it all down to that. And do you know what's happened since you moved in? You've taken her out of herself. That's what you've done. You've taken that girl out of herself.
Smedley (*almost his old self*) Whoops-a-daisy!
James Whoops-a-daisy indeed! So how about a drink!
Smedley Twist my arm.
Iris (*picking up her hat and coat*) I think we could all do with a drink

  Iris goes out into the hall with her things

James pours three whiskys

James Feeling better?

Smedley Fantastic.

James Yes, there's nothing like clearing the air between friends. Here's to you.

Ken All you wish yourself, Jim.

Iris returns

Iris I can't understand it, James. Her coat's still hanging up.

James (*after a pause*) She's gone for a toddle without her coat. It'll do her good. Blow the cobwebs away.

Iris And her walking shoes are in the hall cupboard.

James (*after another pause, uneasily*) She's got her high heels on.

Iris They're in the hall. I very nearly tripped over them.

Smedley rises. They all look at one another

I thought it was funny when we first came in. Her handbag's open on the dressing-table.

James You don't think she could possibly be using the bathroom?

Iris I shouldn't think it's likely.

James It is possible.

Iris Not for this long length of time.

James Perhaps we should look?

Iris goes out into the hall. We hear her knocking on the bathroom door

Iris Marigold? Marigold, love? Are you using the bathroom?

There is a pause. Smedley and James avoid each other's eyes.

Iris rushes in and goes to the telephone

She is in the bathroom.

James Oh, for God's sake!

James hurries out

Iris picks up the telephone and dials nine-nine-nine

Iris (*to Smedley*) She's done it properly this time. (*Into the telephone*) This is seven-five-two six-nine-three-four ... Ambulance, please. (*To Smedley*) She's been taking pills.

James enters

James *We do not* need an ambulance!

Iris (*ignoring him*) This is seven-five-two six-nine-three-four, Mrs Wormald. Could you send an ambulance to Hilltops, The Crescent, off Poplar Grove?

James She's perfectly all right!

Iris, trying to listen to the telephone, glares at James. She snatches the hatchet from his head and throws it down

Iris (*into the telephone*) It's my daughter. She's taken something. She's unconscious. ... Well, they must be pills. ... Yes, I'll see.

Iris rams the telephone into James's hand and rushes out

James looks helplessly at the telephone

James (*to Smedley, apologetically*) She's done it before. It isn't serious.
She's perfectly all right. (*Into the telephone*) My name is Wormald. I'm
the girl's father. I'm afraid my wife is making rather a large mountain
over rather a small . . .

*Iris darts back into the living-room and snatches the telephone from him.
She is holding an aspirin bottle*

Iris Hello? This is Mrs Wormald speaking. They were aspirins. (*To
James, who is glowering at her*) See to her!

James storms out

(*Into the telephone*) The bottle's empty. . . . Yes, very deeply! . . . Yes, I
will. Oh, good. Good. Thank you ever so much.

Over the above we hear James shouting at Marigold in the bathroom

James (*off*) Wake up! Come on, wake up! Marigold! Do you hear me!
How many have you taken! Come on, wake up! Will you bloody wake
up!

Iris (*as she puts down the telephone*) It's no use shouting at her! Who do
you think you're talking to!

Iris rushes out as James storms back in

James picks up his drink and knocks it back. Smedley watches him anxiously

Smedley Will she—er—be all right, do you think?

James Of course she'll be all right! (*Calling to Iris*) There was no need to
call an ambulance! No need at all. (*He downs Iris's drink and turns back
to Smedley, conversationally*) It's not the first time—it won't be the last.
Finish your drink.

Smedley (*setting his glass down*) Not just at this particular moment, Jim.

James Don't be put off by this little oojah-ma-flip.

Iris appears momentarily at the hall door

Iris Help me to get her on her feet!

Iris rushes out again

James turns away impatiently and pours himself another drink

Smedley On my life, Jim, I'd no idea that she was planning anything like
this.

James sips at his drink and studies Smedley, who feels obliged to continue

We . . . We had a long chat. She seemed great. We chewed the fat—this
and that. I mean, I wasn't on the premises for all that length of time.
She was quiet—yes. When I left. Didn't have a great deal to say for herself. But honest to God—on Thelma's life—I'd no idea that she was
planning anything like this.

James (*raising his glass*) First today. (*He drinks*) Sit down! Finish your bloody drink!

Smedley picks up his glass and sits awkwardly

The bloody silly stupid bitch!

Iris appears at the hall door supporting the semi-conscious Marigold

Smedley leaps to his feet

Iris *Help* me with her!

James I'll help her with a boot up the backside.

Iris And stop talking like that. Give me a hand. Help me to try and wake her up.

James goes, grudgingly, and helps Iris to support Marigold. During the following they attempt to walk her about the room

Smedley (*embarrassed*) Look. You don't want me around—intruding. And I really ought to skedaddle, if there's nothing I can do to help . . .

James I've told you what you can do. You can sit down and drink your drink!

Iris (*flashing James an impatient glance*) Marigold? Marigold, dearie? Come along, my love.

James The bloody silly stupid bitch!

Iris Stop it, James! The least you could do is try and show some sympathy!

James She doesn't deserve sympathy! It's her own bloody silly stupid fault!

Iris (*glaring malevolently at Smedley*) It's not her fault—not entirely.

Smedley (*uncomfortably*) What did the ambulance say, Mrs Wormald?

Iris They said to try and walk her about. To try and wake her up.

James You'll be saying next that it's my fault that she's got herself like this?

Iris attempts to ignore him

I suppose it was my fault the last time she did it?

Iris It was different the last time.

James Too bloody true! We didn't have ambulances polling up the street!

Smedley Shouldn't you . . . Isn't there something you should give her? To make her bring it up?

Iris They said not to give her *anything*.

James She doesn't need anything. She's bloody neurotic. That's all that's wrong with her. She waltzed off with Harold—waltzed off with a sexual maniac—because she was neurotic. She's not been married to him five minutes before she waltzes back and does this kind of thing.

Iris You can't blame Harold this time. It's all right, Marigold. It's going to be all right, my love.

James She does it to draw attention to herself.

Iris She's done it because she's unhappy! She's been very unhappy of late.

James Unhappy? She's a raving lunatic.

Iris She's been worried about all kinds of things.

Smedley Perhaps she's had things preying on her mind. Things like divorce and things.

Iris (*stoutly*) The divorce isn't the only thing.

James If that's what's worrying her she can pack it in. Because she's got no chance of getting a divorce.

Iris Of course she's getting a divorce!

James She's got as much chance of getting a divorce as fly, the way she's been carrying on.

Iris She's going to walk into that court and get her divorce, James.

James (*releasing his hold on Marigold*) Walk into court? Look at her! She can't even bloody well stand up!

Iris Hold her, James! Help me to hold her up!

James turns away and it is Smedley who moves forward and helps Iris to support Marigold. Iris is unwilling to accept Smedley's help, but is not in a position to refuse it

(*giving up*) It's no good, isn't this. I'm going to put her into bed until the ambulance comes.

Iris and Smedley stumble out with Marigold

James, apparently unconcerned, watches them go

Smedley re-enters

Smedley We've managed to get her into bed.

James squeezes his squeaky cushion which lets out a loud raspberry

It's a terrible business, Jim.

James It's a bloody tragedy, that's what it is.

Smedley (*fervently*) It is! It is!

James Dirty great ambulance tearing up the street. Lugging her out in front of all the neighbourhood. We'll be the bloody laughing stock. There was no need to fetch the ambulance.

Smedley You'll have to try to keep it quiet. Hush it up.

James Do me a favour, show some sense. Attempted suicide and you say hush it up? We'll have the bobbies on the doorstep next. They'll send for Harold, he's her next of kin. And then the lot comes out—everything. Do you think she stands a chance of getting a divorce—after all this?

Smedley (*carefully*) You see, it's a question of keeping Thelma out of it. And then it's a question of what the neighbours might think.

James To hell with them. I've enough on my plate without worrying about the neighbours.

Smedley We've got to live with them.

James We've got our own lives to live. I've had my bellyful of the neighbours. I've a bloody good mind to pack up and clear off out of it.

Smedley What? Leave the district?

James Get right out of it.

Smedley You can't just pack up and go—can you?

James I can do what I bloody well like.

We hear the ambulance bell as it pulls up outside

Smedley It's here.

James (*pouring himself a large Scotch*) I didn't think it was the ice-bloody-cream van.

Smedley I say—you ought to go a bit easy on that, you know.

James (*dangerously*) Go easy on what?

Smedley The Scotch. You have been caning it a bit today, Jimmy.

James James. I like to be called James. After all it is my bloody name.

Smedley Well—James. I'd give it a bit of a rest if I were you.

James But you're not me, friend. There's only one James Wormald on this planet and I'm he. Copyright reserved. I am the captain of my fate, I am the master of my soul. When I want a bloody drink I'll have a bloody drink, and when I want your bloody advice I'll bloody well ask for it.

Thelma enters from the patio towards the end of James's speech

James raises his glass to her

First today.

Thelma What's the ambulance for?

Smedley Marigold. She's had an accident.

James A bloody self-induced accident. The bloody silly stupid bitch! Have a drink.

Smedley Not just at this immediate moment—thanks.

James Pull your bloody self together, man! Tenshun! Look at him—like a bloody wet blancmange! You say you were in the Engineers? The hard men? (*Slapping his chest*) Royal Army Bloody Pay Corps. One-four-four-three-six-nine-double-one. Corporal Wormald, James. Sir. Four years and nine months in the paymaster's office at Tiverton. Never fired a shot in anger. The bloody Pay Corps, but by Christ it made a better man of me than you'll make in a million years. Get your knees brown. Get some service in. Standing there like a pregnant penguin.

James relishes his drink. Smedley and Thelma are subdued

Iris enters

Iris They're putting her on a stretcher. They *are* going to take her in.

James What do you expect me to do about it?

Iris I want you to come with me, naturally. Down to the hospital.

James Why the hell do you want me?

Iris Because you're her father.

James Bollocks to her.

Iris I can't go on my own, James.

James I see no reason why not.

Iris Because I'm not going out there on my own, that's why not. Not in front of all them.

James All who?

Iris Everybody. Gable-end and Side-by-Side. They've come out in the

gardens. All of them. Rose Cottage has got the baby in her arms—she's
bottle feeding it. And Journey's End is pretending that he's cutting his
hedge.

James finishes his drink and studies the three of them

James Where's my tit-fer? If they want something to talk about I'll give
them it.

Iris gives him his cap and he puts it on

How's that? (*To Iris*) Come on! Get cracking, you dozy bitch.

Iris goes out

James pauses at the door and turns to Smedley and Thelma

Into the Valley of Death rode the six hundred! (*He winks and we see
that he is enjoying the situation*) Whoops-a-daisy! Ken!

*James goes out leaving the hall door open. We hear him berating the
neighbours as he walks down the path*

(*Shouting off*) How-do-you-do? Have you seen everything then? Go
on! Get back in your bloody house, you nosy prying pig! Go on! The
bloody lot of you!

*Smedley and Thelma stand stock-still. We hear the ambulance start up and
drive down the street*

Thelma What happened to him?
Smedley His bottle went.
Thelma What have you done to upset him?
Smedley Nothing!
Thelma (*screaming*) Yes, it's always bloody nothing, isn't it! The best
bloody friends we ever had and you've got to go and bloody needle them!
As per usual! . . . (*She breaks off*)

*Edgar Baldock, a middle-aged mouse of a business man enters cautiously
from the patio*

Baldock I'm terribly sorry to invonvenience you . . .
Smedley Hello?
Baldock I was wondering if I might use your phone.
Smedley Our phone.

Thelma and Smedley are puzzled

Baldock Let me explain. We're moving in next door but one.
Thelma That's next door to us.
Smedley We live next door.
Baldock Then it's not your phone?
Smedley (*extending his hand to the telephone*) It's alla keef. Be my guest.
Jim wouldn't mind.
Baldock (*moving to the telephone*) If you're absolutely sure . . .
Smedley Dead certain.

Baldock I wouldn't trouble you, but it is an emergency. The removal van hasn't arrived.

Smedley Go right ahead.

Baldock turns his back on them and picks up the telephone and dials. Thelma pours three drinks. Smedley picks up the hatchet joke which James discarded, puts it on and tiptoes close to Baldock

Baldock No reply. It really is most aggravating . . . (*He puts down the telephone, turns and starts as he takes in the hatchet joke*)

Smedley Whoops-a-daisy!

Smedley and Thelma go into paroxysms of laughter. After a moment Baldock allows himself an embarrassed giggle. Thelma hands out drinks

You're not a Catholic are you? Well, a quickie . . .

Curtain

FURNITURE AND PROPERTY LIST

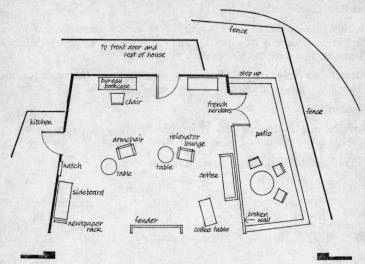

ACT I

SCENE 1

On stage: LIVING-ROOM:

    Settee

    Relaxor lounge

    Upright armchair

    Sideboard. *On it:* telephone, lamp, clock, ornaments. *In cupboards:* bottle of sherry, assorted glasses

    Record player with records in shelf below

    Bureau. *In it:* document. *On shelves above:* books, ornaments, etc.

    Newspaper rack with newspapers, paperbacks, magazines

    Upright chair at bureau

    Low coffee table

    2 occasional tables, one with drawer containing assorted oddments

    Carpet

    Window curtains

    PATIO:

    3 outdoor chairs

    Circular table. *On it:* remains of breakfast for 3 people, including packet of cornflakes, 3 plates, 3 spoons, tray

Off stage: Tray with 4 cups, 4 saucers, 4 teaspoons, teapot, milk jug, sugar bowl, plate of biscuits (**Thelma**)

Personal: **Smedley:** coins

SCENE 2

Strike: Tea things

          Cornflakes

Set: Hammock in patio
Relaxer lounge in new position
Knitting machine on table

Off stage: Bottle of whisky, bottle of gin (Thelma)
Glass of water, tablet (Thelma)
Ringing alarm clock (James)

Personal: Thelma: handbag

ACT II

SCENE 1

Strike: Knitting machine
Used glasses

Set: All drinks back in sideboard
Vacuum cleaner off, with flex leading into bedroom
Several records about room, one on player turntable

Off stage: 2 glasses of Alka-Seltzer (Marigold)
2 shopping bags. *In them:* blazer, corduroy cap (James)
Cine-camera (Smedley)

SCENE 2

Strike: Dressing-gown
Cine-camera

Off stage: Joke hatchet (James)
Carrier-bag with squeaky cushion (James)
Aspirin bottle (Iris)

Personal: James: trick bow-tie, trick pen, trick cigarettes, lighter

LIGHTING PLOT

Property fiittings required: wall brackets, table lamp
Interior. A living-room and patio. The same scene throughout

ACT I, SCENE 1 Morning

To open: General effect of bright morning light

No cues

ACT I, SCENE 2 Evening

To open: Brackets and lamp on. Dusk outside

No cues

ACT II, SCENE 1   Morning
To open: As Act I, Scene 1
No cues

ACT II, SCENE 2   Afternoon
To open: General effect of afternoon daylight
No cues

EFFECTS PLOT

ACT I
SCENE 1

Cue 1	**Iris** exits to kitchen *Doorbell rings*	(Page 7)
Cue 2	**Iris:** ". . . as we always have done." *Telephone rings*	(Page 10)
Cue 3	**Thelma:** "Take two." *Telephone rings*	(Page 15)

SCENE 2

No cues

ACT II
SCENE 1

Cue 4	**Smedley** switches record-player on *Music—"The Merry Widow", Act I, Finale*	(Page 44)
Cue 5	**Marigold** switches record-player off *Music off*	(Page 44)
Cue 6	**Marigold** switches record-player on *Music—"The Merry Widow"—"Love Unspoken"*	(Page 44)
Cue 7	**Marigold** switches record-player off *Music stops*	(Page 44)

SCENE 2

Cue 8	**James:** ". . . what I bloody well like." *Ambulance bell arriving*	(Page 54)
Cue 9	**James** (*off*): "The bloody lot of you!" *Ambulance starting up and driving away*	(Page 56)

MADE AND PRINTED IN GREAT BRITAIN BY
LATIMER TREND & COMPANY LTD PLYMOUTH

MADE IN ENGLAND